ARKANSAS CRIMINAL JUSTICE DIRECTORY 2012-2013

TRIAL COURTS, LAW ENFORCEMENT, AND CORRECTIONS

State, County, City, and Federal

by

John Wesley Hall
Attorney at Law
Little Rock

–and–

Lisa G. Douglas
Attorney at Law
North Little Rock

Note to Readers:

The information in this book was collected from various public and private resources, including Internet searches, public records, and other public and private sources of information, including telephone calls and emails to gather or confirm information. Every effort was made to be certain that all the information in here and correct, but it is inevitable there will be some mistakes in our source documents that we did not notice because there is no other central source document for this information. We did find mistakes in information from our sources, including websites, and corrected them here. We cannot expect that this directory will be completely error-free, but we tried. We also checked election results to show the newly-elected judges. Some elections remain in 2012, and some resignations and replacements will be made.

The cost of this book is underwritten by the advertisements. Douglas is a personal injury lawyer, Hall is a criminal defense lawyer who is a Past President of the National Association of Criminal Defense Lawyers.

Updates and Corrections

If any reader finds mistakes, omissions, or updates that need to be made, please email us at LisaGDouglas@aol.com so the correct or new information can be put in any updates.

This book is published through an "on demand" publication service, so updates can be made more frequently than with other books. It will be updated approximately annually, and you, the readers, will be the best source of new or corrected information.

Acknowledgments

Thanks to all those state, local, and federal officials, deputy clerks, even police communications persons who answered our telephone calls and emails about getting information for this book.

TABLE OF CONTENTS

NOTES

ARKANSAS JUDICIAL DISTRICT MAP

Circuit Judges and Prosecuting Attorneys
Serve These 28 Judicial Districts:

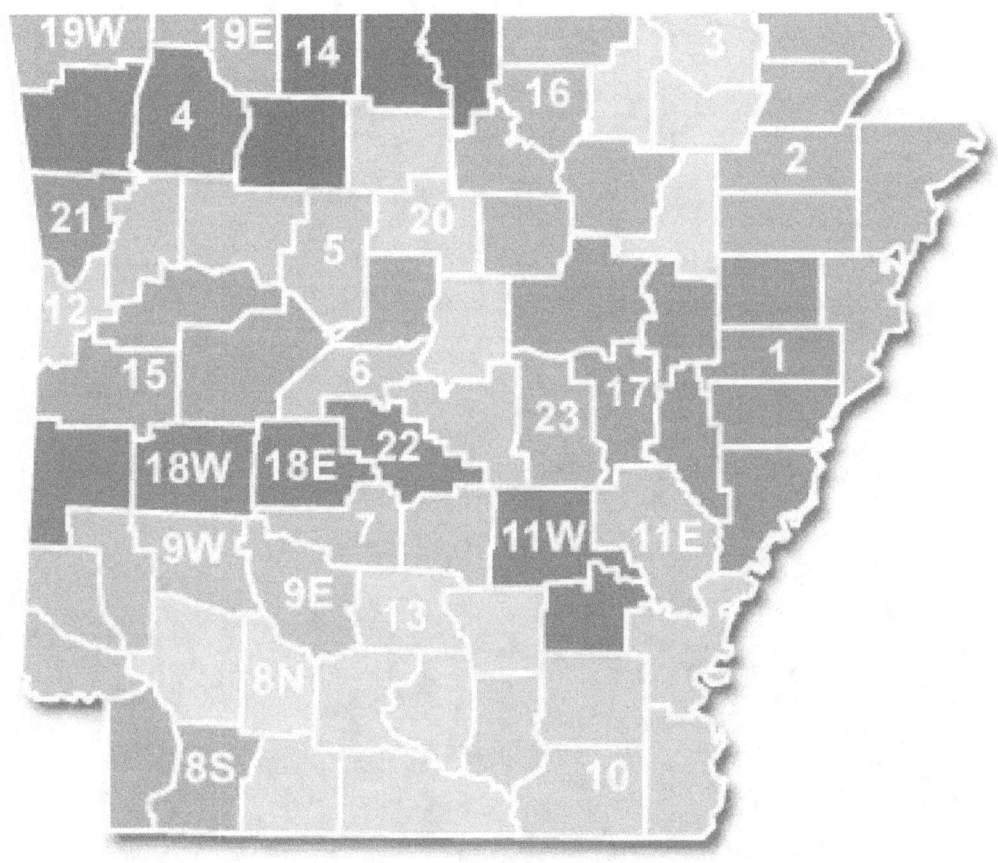

Full Arkansas Judicial Directory on the Arkansas Supreme Court website:
http://courts.state.ar.us/pdf/judicial_directory.pdf

NOTES

Part I:

COURTS
Circuit, District, City, and Federal
and
PROSECUTING ATTORNEYS
State and Federal

NOTES

CIRCUIT JUDGES
(Judicial District map on page 1)

FIRST JUDICIAL CIRCUIT
Cross, Lee, Monroe, Phillips, St. Francis, Woodruff

L.T. Simes – Division 1
P.O. Box 2775   870-338-5518
West Helena   fax 870-335-5591
    Reporter Alvah Griggs // Trial Court Asst. Tiffany Davis

Richard Proctor – Division 2
108 Mississippi Street   870-238-3831
Wynne 72396   fax 870-238-7429
    Reporter Elvetta Stacy // Trial Court Asst. Gwen Bretherick

Ben Story – Division 3
P.O. Box 249   870-261-1740
Forrest City 72336-0249   fax 870-261-1733
    Reporter Carla K. Astin // Trial Court Asst. Yvonne Amos

Kathleen Bell – Division 4
P.O. Box 177   870-338-5522
Helena 72342   fax 870-338-5595
    Reporter Linda Whitfield // Trial Court Asst. Farie Bailey

Ann Hudson – Division 5
P.O. Box 995   870-633-5995
Forrest City 72336   fax 870-630-1203
    Reporter Betty A. McLain // Trial Court Asst. Wonda Smith

SECOND JUDICIAL CIRCUIT
Clay, Craighead, Crittenden, Greene, Mississippi, Poinsett

Pam Honeycutt – Division 1
P.O. Box 1951   870-933-4594
Jonesboro 72403   fax 870-933-7713
    Reporter Michelle Jones // Trial Court Asst. April Rasdon

Lee Fergus – Division 2
P.O. Box 1472
Jonesboro 72403
     Reporter Cynthia D. White // Trial Court Asst. Joyce Morgan

870-933-4548
fax 870-933-7711

Brent Davis – Division 3
P.O. Box 1902
Jonesboro 72403
     Reporter Judy Kincade // Trial Court Asst. Rosemary Jones

870-933-4579
fax 870-933-4596

Cindy Thyer – Division 4
320 West Court Street, Room 212
Paragould 72450
     Reporter Laura Bowen // Trial Court Asst. Belinda Penn

870-239-6308
fax 870-236-4185

Ralph Wilson, Jr. – Division 5
P.O. Box 506
Osceola 72370
     Reporter Sandra Arwood // Trial Court Asst. Billie Bowles

870-563-6035
fax 870-563-6035

Victor Hill – Division 6
P.O. Box 768
West Memphis 72303
     Reporter William Kisselburg //Tr.Ct. Asst. Freddy Whitfield

870-735-0707
fax 870-735-1567

Barbara Halley – Division 7
320 W. Court, Room 210
Paragould 72450
     Reporter Janis Harbuck // Trial Court Asst. Laura Hagen

870-239-6331
fax 870-236-4185

John Fogleman – Division 8
206 River Trace Drive
Marion 72364
     Reporter Elvetta Stacy // Trial Court Asst. Andrea Hicks

870-739-3156
fax 870-933-4596

David Laser – Division 9
P.O. Box 420
Jonesboro 72403
     Reporter Diane Gibson // Trial Court Asst. Brenda Welch

870-933-4599
fax 870-933-7707

Larry Boling – Division 10
P.O. Box 9046
Jonesboro 72403
     Reporter Buffy Topper // Trial Court Asst. Ouida J. Hardin

870-933-4590
fax 870-933-4596

Randy Philhours – Division 11
320 W. Court, Room 226   870-239-6319
Paragould 72450   fax 870-236-4185
    Reporter Jerri Brown // Trial Court Asst. Michelle Grilletta

THIRD JUDICIAL CIRCUIT
Jackson, Lawrence, Randolph, Sharp

Harold Erwin – Division 1
Jackson County Courthouse   870-523-7424
Newport 72112   fax 870-523-7404
    Reporter Rita Wood // Trial Court Asst. Donna Simmons

Philip Smith – Division 2
108 South Marr   870-892-8610
Pocahontas 72455   fax 870-892-9150
    Reporter Joyce King // Trial Court Asst. Chrissie Tanner

Kevin King – Division 3
P.O. Box 477   870-994-3515
Ash Flat 72513   fax 870-994-3516
    Reporter Anita Howard //Trial Court Asst. Geraldine Vaughn

FOURTH JUDICIAL CIRCUIT
Madison, Washington

William Storey – Division 1
P.O. Box 1405   479-444-1560
Fayetteville 72702   fax 479-444-1565
    Reporter Amy Pense // Trial Court Asst. Michele Friend

Kim Smith – Division 2
P.O. Drawer 1206   479-444-1552
Fayetteville 72702-1206   fax 501-444-1752
    Reporter Karen Morrow // Trial Court Asst. Joan Lester

Stacey Zimmerman – Division 3
885 Clydesdale Drive   479-973-8460
Fayetteville 72701   fax 479-444-1749
    Reporter Richard Fourt // Trial Court Asst. Delia Foster

Chad Mason (2012*) – Division 4
P.O. Box 4703   479-973-8420
Fayetteville 72702-4703   fax 479-973-8426
      Reporter Vickie Hassell // Trial Court Asst. Casey Compton
           (two way race for seat in '12)

Beth Storey – Division 5
P.O. Box 1583   479-444-1556
Fayetteville 72702-1583   fax 479-444-1883
      Reporter Add Wood // Trial Court Hannan Ketter

Mark Lindsay – Division 6
P.O. Box 1612   479-444-1548
Fayetteville 72702-1612   fax 479-444-1620
      Reporter Denise Mulliken // Trial Court Asst. Alice Schultz

Joanna Taylor – Division 7
123 North College   479-444-1682
Fayetteville 72701   fax 479-444-1686
      Reporter Shana Leding // Trial Court Asst. Julie Weston

FIFTH JUDICIAL CIRCUIT
Franklin, Johnson, Pope

Bill Pearson – Division 1
P.O. Box 1406   479-754-3495
Clarksville 72830   fax 479-754-5821
      Reporter Johna Roedenbeck // Trial Court Asst. Cindi Sheely

Gordon "Mack" McCain – Division 2
P.O. Box 1124   479-968-2280
Russellville 72811-1124   fax 479-968-6091
      Reporter June Stuart // Trial Court Asst. Meredith Whitson

Ken Coker, Jr. – Division 3
P.O. Box 297   479-968-3869
Russellville 72811-0297   fax 479-880-1810
      Reporter Dianne Satterfield // Trial Court Asst. Erika Grimes

Dennis Sutterfield – Division 4
P.O. Box 249   479-967-5011
Russellville 72811   fax 479-967-6070
      Reporter Willma Vaughn //Trial Court Asst. Michele Matthews

SIXTH JUDICIAL CIRCUIT
Perry, Pulaski

Leon Johnson – Division 1
401 West Markham, Room 420
Little Rock 72201
    501-340-8590
    fax 501-340-6039
        Reporter Amanda Poe // Trial Court Asst. Annette Gilbert

Chris Piazza – Division 2
401 West Markham, Room 230
Little Rock 72201
    501-340-8424
    fax 501-340-8563
        Reporter Debra Westmoreland // Trial Court Asst. Sherri Colbert

James "Jay" Moody – Division 3
401 West Markham, Room 240
Little Rock 72201
    501-340-8426
    fax 501-340-6038
        Reporter Tammie Foreman // Trial Court Asst. Kacie Glenn

Herbert Wright – Division 4
401 West Markham, Room 440
Little Rock 72201
    501-340-8593
    fax 501-340-8822
        Reporter Patricia Toland // Trial Court Asst. Adele Evans

Wendell Griffin – Division 5
401 West Markham, Room 410
Little Rock 72201
    501-340-8550
    fax 501-340-8465
        Ct. Rep. Neva Warford // Trial Court Asst. LaShannon Robinson

Tim Fox – Division 6
401 West Markham, Room 210
Little Rock 72201
    501-340-8416
    fax 501-340-6047
        Reporter Ellen Kuciejski // Trial Court Asst. Christie Greer

Barry Sims – Division 7
401 West Markham, Room 220
Little Rock 72201
    501-340-5630
    fax 501-340-8872
        Reporter Beth Kremers // Trial Court Asst. Karen Cobb

Wiley Branton Jr. – Division 8
3001 W. Roosevelt
Little Rock 72204
    501-340-6666
    fax 501-340-6928
        Reporter Shelley Keeland // Trial Court Asst. Brenda Nellums

Mary McGowan – Division 9
401 West Markham, Room 320   501-340-5602
Little Rock 72201   fax 501-340-5640
   Reporter Melinda Tarver // Trial Court Asst. Jerlene Eason

Joyce Williams Warren – Division 10
3001 W. Roosevelt   501-340-6724
Little Rock 72204   fax 501-340-7016
   Rptr. Meredith Pinkstone // Trial Ct. Asst. Tommi Myers Fell

Beth Branscum Burgess (2012*) – Division 11
3001 W. Roosevelt   501-340-6731
Little Rock 72204   fax 501-340-6931
   Reporter Kathy Begley // Trial Court Asst. Laquina Reed
     (two way race for seat in '12)

Alice Gray – Division 12
401 West Markham, Room 350   501-340-8530
Little Rock 72201   fax 501-340-6035
   Reporter Shiela Russell // Trial Court Asst. Diana Williams

Collins Kilgore – Division 13
401 West Markham, Room 330   501-340-8534
Little Rock 72201   fax 501-340-5625
   Rprtr. Mi Mi Ambrose // Trial Court Asst. AiLien Draheim

Vann Smith – Division 14
401 West Markham, Room 300   501-340-8538
Little Rock 72201   fax 501-340-6036
   Reporter Ranaye Cameron // Trial Court Asst. Melissa King

Richard Moore – Division 15
401 West Markham, Room 340   501-340-5610
Little Rock 72201   fax 501-340-6037
   Reporter Ellen Hart // Trial Court Asst. Julie Moory

Ellen Brantley (thru '12); Morgan Welch ('13-'18) – Division 16
401 West Markham, Room 310   501-340-8542
Little Rock 72201   fax 501-340-6034
   Reporter Amber Speer // Trial Court Asst. Rosie Talbort

Mackie Pierce – Division 17
401 West Markham, Room 360   501-340-5620
Little Rock 72201   fax 501-340-5657
     Reporter Maria Lafferty // Trial Court Asst. Rose Sykes

SEVENTH JUDICIAL CIRCUIT
Grant, Hot Spring

Chris Williams – Division 1
Hot Springs County Courthouse
Locust & Second Streets   501-337-7651
Malvern 72104   fax 501-337-7744
     Reporter Leca Ledbetter // Trial Court Asst. Linda Simmonds

Edward M. Koon (2012, Eddy Easley, '13-'14) – Division 2
Grant County Courthouse, Room 109
101 W. Center   870-942-7818
Sheridan 72150   fax 870-942-1622
     Reporter Marguret Lancaster // Trial Court. Asst. Darlene Walters

EIGHTH NORTH JUDICIAL CIRCUIT
Hempstead, Nevada

Randy Wright – Division 1
P.O. Box 621   870-777-4544
Hope 71801   fax 870-777-6568
     Reporter Donna Watkins // Trial Court Asst. Janis Porterfield

Duncan Culpepper – Division 2
P.O. Box 605   870-887-8787
Prescott 71856-0605   fax 870-887-3208
     Reporter Amy May // Trial Court Asst. Kit Lucena

EIGHTH SOUTH JUDICIAL CIRCUIT
Lafayette, Miller

Joe Griffin – Division 1
Courthouse
400 Laurel Street, Suite 201   870-774-2421
Texarkana 71854   fax 870-772-4680
     Reporter Jewell Benson // Trial Court Asst. Jodi Burke

Brent Haltom – Division 2
Courthouse
400 Laurel Street, Suite 202   870-772-9618
Texarkana 71854   fax 870-773-3354
        Reporter Frances Haynes// Trial Court Asst. Karen Goodrum

Kirk Johnson – Division 3
Courthouse
400 Laurel Street, Suite 304   870-774-7722
Texarkana 71854   fax 870-774-0008
        Reporter Tabbetha Kopech // Trial Court Asst. Lisa Houser

NINTH EAST JUDICIAL CIRCUIT
Clark

Robert McCallum – Division 1
P.O. Box 966   870-246-8218
Arkadelphia 71923   fax 870-246-9378
        Reporter Jacqueline Marvin // Trial Court Asst. Lanna Clark

NINTH WEST JUDICIAL CIRCUIT
Howard, Little River, Pike, Sevier

Tom Cooper – Division 1
P.O. Box 214   870-898-7228
Ashdown 71822   fax 870-898-7262
        Reporter Kim Garner // Trial Court Asst. Martha Williams

Charles Yeargan – Division 2
P.O. Box 820   870-285-2900
Murfreesboro 71958   fax 870-285-2950
        Reporter Chren Kesterson // Trial Court Asst. Linda Ballard

TENTH JUDICIAL CIRCUIT
Ashley, Bradley, Chicot, Desha, Drew

Sam Pope – Division 1
Courthouse
215 East Jefferson   870-853-2032
Hamburg 71646   fax 870-853-2032
        Reporter Mike Ashcraft // Trial Court Asst. Pam Murphy

Kenny Johnson – Division 2
Bradley County Courthouse
101 East Cedar   870-226-4420
Warren 71671   fax 870-226-4424
          Reporter Jan McLemore // Trial Court Asst. JoAnn Smith

Bynum Gibson – Division 3
Drew County Courthouse   870-367-7604
Monticello 71655   fax 870-367-2092
          Rptr. Sherry Parker-East // Trial Court Asst. Penny Rosegrant

Don Glover – Division 4
P.O. Box 398   870-222-6885
McGehee 71654   fax 870-222-4781
          Reporter Margaret Norton // Trial Court Asst. Helen King

Teresa French – Division 5
P.O. Box 50   870-222-6598
McGehee 71654   fax 870-222-6597
          Reporter Bobby Reynolds // Trial Court Asst. Laura Berryman

ELEVENTH EAST JUDICIAL CIRCUIT
Arkansas

David Henry – Division 1
P.O. Box 1166   870-673-3181
Stuttgart 72160   fax 870-673-1168
          Reporter Stacey Simpson // Trial Court Asst. Mindy Hoskyn

ELEVENTH WEST JUDICIAL CIRCUIT
Jefferson, Lincoln

Berlin Jones – Division 1
Jefferson County Courthouse
108 E. Barraque Suite 212   870-541-5368
Pine Bluff 71611   fax 870-540-5370
          Reporter Docie Johnson // Trial Court Asst. Jerrie Dean

Robert Wyatt, Jr. – Division 2
Jefferson County Courthouse
101 W. Barraque, Room 216, P.O. Box 9140   870-541-5465
Pine Bluff 71611   fax 870-541-5337
     Reporter Jerry Lawson // Trial Court Asst. Sarah Miller

William Benton – Division 3
Courthouse
108 East Barraque, Suite 212   870-541-5381
Pine Bluff 71601   fax 870-541-5380
     Reporter Nancy Lindsay // Trial Court Asst. Lisa Stewart

Leon Jamison – Division 4
Courthouse
101 West Barraque, Room 204   870-541-5383
Pine Bluff 71611   fax 870-541-5385
     Reporter Nevelyn Smith // Trial Court Asst. Diane Duncan

Jodi Dennis – Division 5
101 W Barraque, Room 210, P.O. Box 8705   870-541-5377
Pine Bluff 71601   fax 870 536-2776
     Reporter Sharon Moody // Trial Court Asst. Kim Taylor

Earnest E. Brown – Division 6
301 E. Second Street, P.O. Box 6116   870-541-5461
Pine Bluff 71611   fax 870-541-5464
     Reporter Pat Works// Trial Court Asst. Carla Wooley

TWELFTH JUDICIAL CIRCUIT
Sebastian

Steve Tabor – Division 1
Sebastian County Courts Bldg.
901 S. "B" Street   479-782-4715
Fort Smith 72901   fax 479-784-1527
     Reporter Monica Kinney // Trial Court Asst. Janet Smith

Annie Hendricks – Division 2
Sebastian County Courts Bldg.
901 S. "B" Street   479-782-0394
Fort Smith 72901   fax 479-784-1539
     Reporter Brenda Thompson // Trial Court Asst. Gayla Moses

Jim Spears – Division 3
Sebastian County Courts Bldg.
901 S. "B" Street 479-784-1560
Fort Smith 72901 fax 479-784-1563
  Reporter Ronda Brown // Trial Court Asst. Barbara Reed

Mark Hewlett – Division 4
Sebastian County Courts Bldg.
901 S. "B" Street 479-783-1721
Fort Smith 72901 fax 479-784-1543
  Reporter Lavern Ball // Trial Court Asst. Jeannette Langham

J. Michael Fitzhugh – Division 5
Sebastian County Courts Bldg.
901 S. "B" Street 479-782-8667
Fort Smith 72901 fax 479-784-1566
  Reporter Bill Mauldin // Trial Court Asst. Janie T. Evitts

James Cox – Division 6
Sebastian County Courts Bldg.
901 S. "B" Street 479-782-3035
Fort Smith 72901 fax 479-784-1537
  Reporter Paula Sparrow // Trial Court Asst. Kim Dodson

Trial Court Administrator (criminal cases) – Denora Coomer 479-783-1103
dcommer@co.sebastian.ar.us fax 479-784-1013

THIRTEENTH JUDICIAL CIRCUIT
Calhoun, Cleveland, Columbia, Dallas, Ouachita, Union

Hamilton Singleton – Division 1
Courthouse
P.O. Box 763 870-837-2272
Camden 71701 fax 870-837-2271
  Reporter Rosemary Richerdson// Trial Ct. Asst. Linda Wolfe

Mike Landers – Division 2
Courthouse, Room 303 870-864-1937
El Dorado 71730 fax 870-864-1966
  Reporter Linda Sue Bell // Trial Court Asst. Vickie Evans

Edwin Keaton – Division 3
Courthouse
Camden 71701
Reporter Alice Murphy // Trial Court Asst. Tonja Avery

870-837-2270
fax 870-837-2273

Searcy W. Harrell, Jr. (2012, (Robin J. Carroll, '13-'18, El Dorado) – Division 4
Ouachita County Detention Center
109 Goodgame Street
Camden 71701
Reporter Felisha Burson // Trial Court Asst. Becky Gilbert

870-231-9145
fax 870-231-9330

Larry Chandler – Division 5
P.O. Box 785
Magnolia 71753
Reporter Jerri Gale Harrelson // Trial Court Asst. Rebecca Drake

870-235-3781
fax 870-235-3780

David Guthrie – Division 6
Union County Courthouse, Room 205
El Dorado 71730
Reporter Paulette Wright // Trial Court Asst. Verna Clark

870-864-1968
fax 870-864-1969

FOURTEENTH JUDICIAL CIRCUIT
Baxter, Boone, Marion, Newton

Shawn A. Womack – Division 1
301 East 6th Street, Suite 201
Mountain Home 72653
Reporter Megan Lair // Trial Court Asst. Claudette Davis

870-424-5000
fax 870-424-5500

Gary Isbell – Division 2
301 East 6th Street, Suite 154
Mountain Home 72653
Reporter Rebecca Burnham // Trial Court Asst. Janette Pedigo

870-425-8625
fax 870-425-8630

John Putman – Division 3
Courthouse, Room 305
100 North Main
Harrison 72601
Reporter Monica Harper// Trial Court Asst. Eunie Dunkin

870-741-3800
fax 870-741-2563

Gordon Webb – Division 4
Courthouse, Room 301
101 N. Main, P.O. Box 785   870-741-2102
Harrison 72602   fax 870-741-1874
    Reporter Ralenne McBee // Trial Court Asst. Polly Leimberg

FIFTEENTH JUDICIAL CIRCUIT
Conway, Logan, Scott, Yell

Jerry Don Ramey – Division 1
117 South Moose, Room 303   479-354-9620
Morrilton 72110   fax 479-354-9650
    Reporter Larry Shepherd // Trial Court Asst. Hope Millsap

David McCormick – Division 2
108 Union Street, Room 108   479-229-3580
Dardanelle 72834   fax 479-229-1095
    Reporter Glenda Vaughn // Trial Court Asst. Melinda Piatt

Terry Sullivan – Division 3
P.O. Box 400   479-495-7975
Danville 72833   fax 479-495-2607
    Reporter Joyce Woolf // Trial Court Asst. Becky Sexton

SIXTEENTH JUDICIAL CIRCUIT
Cleburne, Fulton, Independence, Izard, Stone

John Dan Kemp – Division 1
Courthouse
P.O. Box 329   870-269-8989
Mountain View 72560   fax 870-269-8964
    Rprtr. Leigh Coffman// Trial Court Asst. Ruth Bonds and

                               Barbara Kuhn

Adam Harkey – Division 2
Courthouse
P.O. Box 2656   870-793-8890
Batesville 72503   fax 870-793-8813
    Reporter Linda Hubbard // Trial Court Asst. Melissa Anderson

Lee Harrod – Division 3
Courthouse
P.O. Box 1421
Heber Springs 72543
     Reporter Megan Wood // Trial Court Asst. Tonya Benton

501-793-8809
fax 501-362-4646

Tim Weaver – Division 4
Courthouse
P.O. Box 1361
Melbourne 72556
     Reporter Fan Dozier // Trial Court Asst. Martha Fleming

870-368-3640
fax 870-368-7457

SEVENTEENTH JUDICIAL CIRCUIT
Prairie, White

Tom Hughes – Division 1
Wilbur Mills Courts Building
301 West Arch
Searcy 72143
     Reporter Vickie Foster // Trial Court Asst. Francis Robin

501-279-6219
fax 501-279-6218

Robert Edwards – Division 2
1600 E. Booth, Suite 500
Searcy 72143
     Reporter Reni Irby// Trial Court Asst. Connie Newkirk

501-279-6212
fax 501-279-6293

Craig Hannah – Division 3
Courthouse
300 North Spruce Street
Searcy 72143
     Reporter Linda Goforth // Trial Court Asst. Brenda Landis

501-279-6221
fax 501-279-6224

EIGHTEENTH EAST JUDICIAL CIRCUIT
Garland

John Homer Wright – Division 1
Courthouse, Room 301
Hot Springs 71901
     Reporter Shari Hamilton // Trial Court Asst. Sherri Daniels

501-321-1333
fax 501-623-5149

Vicki Cook – Division 2
607 Ouachita Avenue
Hot Springs 71901
Reporter Rene Hebert Daugherty // Trial Court Asst. Sarah Beaty

501-622-3770
fax 501-321-0067

Lynn Williams – Division 3
Courthouse, Room 203
Hot Springs 71901
Reporter Melissa Baber // Trial Ct. Asst. Bridgette Howard

501-622-3755
fax 501-622-3629

Marcia Hearnsberger – Division 4
Courthouse, Room 303
Hot Springs 71901
Reporter Jana Hawley // Trial Court Asst. Cindy Hunt

501-622-3760
fax 501-662-3605

EIGHTEENTH WEST JUDICIAL CIRCUIT
Montgomery, Polk

J.W. ("Jake") Looney – Division 1
Courthouse, Room 203
507 Church Street
Mena 71953
Reporter Mary Dixon // Trial Court Asst. Michelle Boehler

479-394-8107
fax 479-394-8109

NINETEENTH EAST JUDICIAL CIRCUIT
Carroll

Kent Crow – Division 1
P.O. Drawer 231
Berryville 72616
Reporter Laura Carnahan // Trial Court Asst. Nadine Holland

870-423-7131
fax 870-423-5824

NINETEENTH WEST JUDICIAL CIRCUIT
Benton

Robin Green – Division 1
Courthouse
100 Northeast "A" Street
Bentonville 71712
Reporter Katherine Pierson // Trial Court Asst. Terri Womack

479-271-1026
fax 479-271-5708

Jon Comstock (2012, Brad Karren 2013–) – Division 2
Courthouse Annex
201 Northeast Second St.   479-271-1063
Bentonville 72712   fax 479-271-1050
    Reporter Sharon Fields // Trial Court Asst. Donna Fleer

Mark Fryauf (2012, Tom Smith 2013–)– Division 3
Courthouse
102 Northeast "A" Street Box 2   479-271-1020
Bentonville 72712   fax 479-271-5752
    Reporter Janis McLeod // Trial Court Asst. Bonnie Ridley

John Scott (2012*)– Division 4
Courthouse
102 Northeast "A" Street Box 12   479-271-1022
Bentonville 72712   fax 479-271-5750
    Reporter Therese Olenberger // Trial Court Asst. Betty Schrader
        (two way race in Fall 2012)

Xollie Duncan – Division 5
Courthouse
102 Northeast "A" Street Room 309   479-271-1024
Bentonville 72712   fax 479-271-5706
    Reporter Cathy Gardisser// Trial Court Asst. Teresa Rich

Dough Schrantz – Division 6
202 East Central   479-464-6114
Bentonville 72712   fax 479-464-6116
    Reporter Darlene Young // Trial Court Asst. Chea Ball

TWENTIETH JUDICIAL CIRCUIT
Faulkner, Searcy, Van Buren

David Reynolds (2012, elected to D.C. 2013–) – Division 1
Courthouse
801 Locust Street   501-450-4925
Conway 72034   fax 501-450-4966
    Reporter Deborah Whillock // Trial Court Asst. Ginger Hall
        (must resign, replacement to be appointed by Governor)

Mike Maggio – Division 2
Courthouse
801 Locust Street   501-450-4904
Conway 72034   fax 501-450-4977
        Reporter Mary May // Trial Court Asst. Susan McGehee

Charles E. Clawson, Jr. – Division 3
Courthouse
801 Locust Street   501-450-4970
Conway 72034   fax 501-450-4972
        Reporter Beth Vint // Trial Court Asst. Kim Gary

David Clark – Division 4
Courthouse
801 Locust Street   501-328-4156
Conway 72034   fax 501-328-4157
        Reporter Gloria Nickles // Trial Court Asst. Shannon Nylor

Rhonda Wood (2012, Elected to Court of Appeals 2013–) – Division 5
1423 Caldwell   501-450-4931
Conway 72034   fax 501-329-4934
        Reporter Julie Beckman // Trial Court Asst. Linda Ahlen
             (replacement to be appointed by Governor)

TWENTY-FIRST JUDICIAL CIRCUIT
Crawford

Gary Cottrell – Division 1
County Courthouse, Room 25
300 Main Street   479-474-6332
Van Buren 72956   fax 479-471-3212
        Reporter Joan Douglas // Trial Court Asst. Vickie Jones

Mike Medlock – Division 2
220 South 4th   479-471-3290
Van Buren 72956   fax 479-471-3292
        Reporter Nancy Warren // Trial Court Asst. Linda Walker

TWENTY-SECOND JUDICIAL CIRCUIT
Saline

Bobby D. McCallister – Division 1
200 North Main Suite 105   501-303-5635
Benton 72015   fax 501-303-5636
    Reporter Amber White // Trial Court Asst. Marcey Lawson

Gary Arnold – Division 2
Saline County Courthouse
200 North Main   501-303-5664
Benton 72015   fax 501-303-5695
    Reporter Jan Brooks // Trial Court Asst. Midge Snow

Grisham Phillips – Division 3
200 North Main   501-303-5628
Benton 72015   fax 501-303-5629
    Reporter Linda Dyer // Trial Court Asst. Lisa Graves

Robert Herzfeld – Division 4
Courthouse Annex
321 N. Main   501-303-1584
Benton 72015   fax 501-303-1585
    Reporter Valarie Flora // Trial Court Asst. Andrea Pate

TWENTY-THIRD JUDICIAL CIRCUIT
Lonoke

Barbara Elmore – Division 1
Courthouse
301 North Center, Suite 303   501-676-3131
Lonoke 72086   fax 501-676-3034
    Reporter Krystal Jones // Trial Court Asst. Deseria Blair

Phillip Whiteaker – Division 2
Courthouse
301 North Center, Suite 302   501-676-3007
Lonoke 72086   fax 501-676-3059
    Reporter Donna Wood // Trial Court Asst. James Tapscott

Sandy Huckabee – Division 3
Courthouse
301 North Center, Suite 101
Lonoke 72086
Reporter Kathy Minton // Trial Court Asst. Margaret Uzzell

501-676-3090
fax 501-676-3093

CIRCUIT CLERKS

Notes: (1) Judicial Districts (map on page 1) under County name; (2) the County's number follows county name for case numbers; (3) all are in courthouses, court buildings, or across the street; (4) email addresses were sought for all, but not all provided one.

Arkansas – 1 11E	Sarah Merchant 101 Court Square DeWitt 72042.	arcocircuitclerk@ymail.com 870-946-4219 fax 870-946-1394
	302 S. College St. Stuttgart 72160	870-673-2056 fax 870-673-3869
Ashley – 2 10	Vickie Stell 205 East Jefferson Hamburg 71646	vstell4@sbcglobal.net 870-853-2030 fax 870-853-2034
Baxter – 3 14	Rhonda Porter One East 7th Mt. Home 72653	baxterclerk@centurytel.net 870-425-3475 fax 870-424-5105
Benton – 4 19W	Brenda DeShields 102 Northeast "A" St. Bentonville 72712	hdeshields@co.benton.ar.us 479-271-1015 479-271-5719
Boone – 5 14	Jeannie Steen 100 North Main Harrison 72601	jsteen@boonecounty-ar.gov 870-741-5560 fax 870-741-4335
Bradley – 5 10	Cindy Wagnon 101 East Cedar Warren 71671.	870-226-2272 fax 870-226-8404
Calhoun – 6 13	Alma Davis P.O. Box 1175 Hampton 71744	hogskinholidays@hotmail.com 870-798-2517 fax 870-798-2428
Carroll – 7 19E	Ramona Wilson 210 W. Church Ave. Berryville 72616	ramonacircuitclerk@gmail.com 870-423-2422 fax 870-423-4796

| | 44 S. Main | 479-253-8646 |
| | Eureka Springs 72632 .... | fax 479-253-6013 |

Chicot – 8
10

Josephine T. Griffin	jgriffinchicotcc@att.net
108 Main Street	870-265-8010
Lake Village 71653.	fax 870-265-8012

Clark – 9
9E

Martha Jo Smith	martha@clarkcountyarkansas.com
Courthouse Square	870-246-4281
Arkadelphia 71923	fax 870-246-1419

Clay – 10
2

Janet Luff Kilbreath	claycce@centurytel.net
151 S. Second Ave.	870-598-2524
Piggott 72454	fax 870-598-1107

| 800 W. 2nd St. | 870-857-3271 |
| Corning 72422 .... | fax 870-857-9201 |

Cleburne – 11
16

Karen Giles	
301 West Main St.	501-362-8149
Heber Springs 72543.	fax 501-362-4650

Cleveland –12
13

Sharon Gray	clevelandclerk@arkansasclerks.com
P.O. Box 368	870-325-6521
Rison, 71665-0368	fax 870-324-6144

Columbia – 13
13

Janice Linkous	circuitclerk@countyofcolumbia.net
One Court Square	870-235-3700
Magnolia 71753	fax 870-235-3786

Conway – 14
15

Darlene Massingill	circlrk@conwaycounty.org
115 S. Moose St.	501-354-9617
Morrilton 72110...............................	fax 501-354-9612

Craighead –15
2

Ann Hudson	ahudson@craigheadcounty.org
511 S. Main St.	870-933-4530
Jonesboro 72401	fax 870-933-4534

Lesia Couch	
P.O. Box 537	870-237-4342
Lake City 72437	fax 870-237-8174

Crawford – 16 Sharon Blount   sblount@crawford-county.org
21   300 Main Street   479-474-1821
               Van Buren 72956 . . . . fax 479-471-0622

Crittenden –17 Terry Hawkins   critcircl@crittco.com
2   100 Court Street   870-739-3248
               Marion 72364 . . . . fax 870-739-3287

Cross – 18   Rhonda J. Sullivan   sullivantrio@yahoo.com
1   705 E. Union   870-238-5720
               Wynne 72396 . . . . fax 870-238-5722

Dallas – 19   Susie Williams   susie09co_cir@windstream.net
13   202 3rd Street West   870-352-2307
               Fordyce 71742. . . . . fax 870-352-7179

Desha – 20   Skippy Leek   slcircuitclerk@deshacounty.org
10   P.O. Box 309   870-877-2411
               Arkansas City 71630 . . . . fax 870-877-3407

Drew – 21   Pat Savage   drewclerk@arkansasclerks.com
10   210 South Main   870-460-6250
               Monticello 71655 . . . . fax 870-460-6255

Faulkner – 23 Rhonda S.L. Wharton   rwharton@faulknercounty.org
20   724 Locust Street   501-450-4913
               Conway 72034. . . . . fax 501-450-4948

Franklin – 24 Wilma Brushwood   franklincocircuit@centurytel.net
5   P.O. Box 1112   479-667-3818
               Ozark 72949 . . . . fax 479-667-5174

               607 E. Main St.   479-965-7332
               Charleston 72933. . . . . fax 870-965-9322

Fulton – 25   Vickie Bishop   vickiefcclerk@centurytel.net
16   P.O. Box 219   870-895-3310
               Salem 72576-0219 . . . . fax 870-895-3383

Garland – 26   Jeannie Pike   vicki@garlandcounty.org
18E   501 Ouachita   501-622-3630
               Hot Springs 71901 . . . . fax 501-609-9043

Grant – 27	Carol Ewing	gcclerk@seark.net
7	101 W. Center, Rm. 106	870-942-2631
	Sheridan 72150	fax 870-942-3564
Greene – 28	Jan Griffin	greenecirclerk@paragould.net
2	3d & Court Streets	870-239-6330
	Paragould 72450..	fax 870-239-3550
Hempstead	Gail Wolfenbarger	hepsteadclerk@arkansasclerks.com
– 29	P.O. Box 1420	870-777-2384
8N	Hope 71801-1420	fax 870-777-7827
Hot Spring –30	Mayme Brown	sjones@hotspringcounty.org
7	210 Locust Street	501-332-2281
	Malvern 72104	fax 501-332-2221
Howard – 31	Bobby Jo Green	bobbie.jo.green@arkansas.gov
9W	421 N. Main St.	870-845-7506
	Nashville 71852	fax 870-845-7505
Indepen-	Deborah Finley	incirfines@swbell.net
dence – 32	192 E. Main St.	870-793-8833
16	Batesville 72501.	fax 870-793-8888
Izard – 33	Rhonda Halbrook	izardclerk@arkansasclerks.com
16	Main & Lunen Sts.	870-368-4316
	Melbourne 72556	fax 870-368-4748
Jackson – 34	Lisa Turner	pamdgram@yahoo.com
3	208 Main Street	870-523-7423
	Newport 72112	fax 870-523-3682
Jefferson – 35	Lafayette Woods	
11W	101 W. Barraque St.	870-541-5311
	Pine Bluff 71601	fax 870-870-5453
Johnson – 36	Jane Houston	jcccjane@centurytel.com
5	Main Street, P.O. Box 189	479-754-2977
	Clarksville 72830..	fax 479-754-4235
Lafayette – 37	Mary Jo Rogers	lafcocirclerk@whti.net
8S	#3 Courthouse Square	870-921-4878
	Lewisville 71845	fax 870-921-4879

Lawrence – 38 3	Michelle Evans Courthouse, P.O. Box 581 Walnut Ridge 72476	lawcocircuit@yahoo.com 870-886-1112 fax 870-886-1128
Lee – 39 1	Mary Ann Wilkinson 15 East Chestnut Marianna 72360	maryannwilkinson1@att.net 870-295-7710 fax 870-295-7712
Lincoln – 40 11W	Vera B. Reynolds 300 S. Drew Star City 71667	lincocircuitclerk@centurytel.net 870-628-3154 fax 870-628-5546
Little River – 41 9W	Andrea Billingsley 351 N. Second St. Ashdown 71822	lrcircuitclerk@lit.countyservice.net 870-898-7211 fax 870-898-5783
Logan – 42 15	Everly Kellar 25 West Walnut Paris 72855 . . . . Courthouse Booneville 72927.	 479-963-2164 fax 479-963-3304 479-675-2894 fax 479-675-0577
Lonoke – 43 23	Denise Brown 301 North Center St., P.O. Box 188 Lonoke 72086	dinglesby@yahoo.com 501-676-2316 fax 501-676-3014
Madison – 44 4	Phyllis Villines P.O. Box 626 Huntsville 72740.	mccourt@madisoncounty.net 479-738-2215 fax 479-738-1544
Marion – 45 14	Dee Carlton P.O. Box 385 Yellville 72687.	clerkmarioncounty@yahoo.com 870-449-6226 fax 870-449-4979
Miller – 46 8	Mary Pankey 412 Laurel St., Suite 109 Texarkana 71854.	 870-774-4501 fax 870-772-5293
Mississippi – 47 2	Donna Bray P.O. Box 1498 Blytheville 72316	m_star_vert@yahoo.com 870-762-2332 fax 870-762-8148

| | P.O. Box 466 | 870-563-6471 |
| | Osceola 72370 . . . . | fax 870-563-5063 |

| Monroe – 48
1 | Alice F. Smith
123 Madison
Clarendon 72029 . . . . | mccirclerk@centurytel.net
870-747-3615
fax 870-747-3710 |

| Mont-
gomery – 49
18W | Debbie Baxter
105 Hwy 270 E #10
Mount Ida 71957   . . . . | montgomeryclerk@arkansasclerks.com
870-867-3521
fax 870-867-2177 |

| Nevada – 50
8 | Rita Reyenga
215 E. 2d Street
Prescott 71857 . . . . | ritareyenga@hotmail.com
870-887-2511
fax 870-887-1911 |

| Newton – 51
14 | Donnie Davis
P.O. Box 410
Jasper 72641 . . . . | newtonclerk@arkansasclerks.com
870-446-5125
fax 870-446-5755 |

| Ouachita – 52
13 | Betty R. Wilson
145 Jefferson S.W.
Camden 71701 . . . . | 870-837-2230
fax 870-837-2252 |

| Perry – 53
6 | Persundra Hood
P.O. Box 358
Perryville 72126 . . . . | blovell@arbbs.net
501-889-5126
fax 501-889-5759 |

| Phillips – 54
1 | Lynn Stillwell
620 Cherry #206
Helena 72342 . . . . | 870-338-5515
fax 870-338-5513 |

| Pike – 55
9W | Donna White
P.O. Box 219
Murfreesboro 71958 . . . . | pikedwhite@windstream.net
870-285-2231
fax 870-285-3281 |

| Poinsett – 56
2 | Claudia Matthews
401 Market Street
Harrisburg 72432 . . . . | 870-578-4420
fax 870-578-4427 |

| Polk – 57
18W | Sharon Simmons
507 Church Street
Mena 71953. . . . . | sharon.circuit@sbcglobal.net
479-394-8100
fax 479-394-8170 |

Pope – 58 5	Fern Tucker 100 W Main Russellville 72801	ferntucker@hotmail.com 479-968-7499 fax 479-880-8463
Prairie – 59 17	Janell Taylor 200 Courthouse Sq., #104 Des Arc 72040	prairieclerk@arkansasclerks.com 870-256-4434 fax 870-256-4434
	P.O. Box 283 DeValls Bluff 72041	870-998-2314 fax 870-998-2314
Pulaski – 60 6	Larry Crane 401 West Markham Little Rock 72201	jbryant@pulaskiclerk.com www.pulaskiclerk.com 501-340-8431 fax (civil/criminal) 501-340-8420

Pulaski – 60 6

Larry Crane
401 West Markham
Little Rock 72201
     jbryant@pulaskiclerk.com
     www.pulaskiclerk.com
     501-340-8431
     fax (civil/criminal) 501-340-8420

Court Administrator
Steve Sipes
     501-340-8411
401 West Markham, Room 120 . . . . fax 501-340-8340

Central Receiving, Room 120
     mhenry@pulaskiclerk.com
New suits and Pleadings (all cases)
Orders of Protection
Administrative and Appeals from lower court. 501-340-8412

Court Records, Room 103
     icrenshaw@pulaskiclerk.com
Maintenance of all Circuit Court case files
Initiation of Petitions to Seal
Certified Copies. 501-340-8766

Appeal Transcripts 501-340-8431
Data Entry I (Div. 1-7)
     kmitteer@pulaskiclerk.com
Expungements

Data Entry II (Div. 9, 12-17). 501-340-8411
OCSE
     bhonorable-phillips@pulaskiclerk.com
Orders of Income Withholding (Support)

Juvenile (Div. 8,10,11)
     bstewart@pulaskiclerk.com
3001 W. Roosevelt
Little Rock 72204. 501-340-6767

Involuntary Commitments / Intake
4710 W. Seventh Street
     501-686-9191
Little Rock 72205. . . . . fax 501-686-9442

	Real Estate	kglenn@pulaskiclerk.com
	Recording, Room 216..............................	501-340-8433
Randolph – 61 3	Debbie Wise 107 W. Broadway Pocahontas 72455...............................	randolphcircuitclerk@yahoo.com 870-892-5522 fax 870-892-8794
St. Francis –62 1	Bette S. Green 313 South Izard Forrest City 72335	BetteSGreen@cablelynx.com 870-261-1715 fax 870-261-1723
Saline – 63 22	Dennis Milligan 200 N. Main St. Benton 72015	dkidd@salinecounty.org 501-303-5615 fax – none
Scott – 64 15	Sandra Staggs 100 West 1st St. Box 10 Waldron 72958	scottcountyclerk@yahoo.com 479-637-2642 fax 479-637-0124
Searcy – 65 20	Debbi Loggins P.O. Box 998 Marshall 72650	searcyclerk@arkansasclerks.com 870-448-3807 fax 870-448-5005
Sebastian –66 12	Kevin Blevins Sebastian County Courts Bldg 901 S. "B" St. Fort Smith 72902	cgilmer@co.sebastian.ar.us 479-782-1046 fax 479-784-1580
	P.O. Box 310 Greenwood 72936	479-996-4175 fax 479-996-6885
Sevier – 67 9W	Patti Chaney 115 N. 3rd St. DeQueen 71832	sccirclk@windstream.net 870-584-3055 fax 870-642-3119
Sharp – 68 3	Tommy Estes P.O. Box 307 Ash Flat 72513................................	sharpclerk@arkansasclerks.com 870-994-7361 fax 870-994-7712
Stone – 69 16	Donna Wilson HC 71, Box 1 Mountain View 72560	djwilson@mvtel.net 870-269-3271 fax 870-269-2303

| Union – 70 13 | Cheryl Wilson 101 N. Washington El Dorado 71730 . . . . | cewilson@hotmail.com 870-864-1940 fax 870-864-1994 |

Union – 70
13

Cheryl Wilson
101 N. Washington
El Dorado 71730 . . . .

cewilson@hotmail.com
870-864-1940
fax 870-864-1994

Van Buren –71
20

Ester Bass
451 Main Street
Clinton 72031 . . . .

501-745-4140
fax 501-745-7400

Washing-
ton – 72
4

Bette Stamps
Washington County Courts Building
280 N. College, Room 302
Fayetteville 72701 . . . .

bstamps@co.washington.ar.us

479-444-1538
fax 479-444-1537

White – 73
17

Tami King
300 N. Spruce
Searcy 72143 . . . .

whitecountyclerk@cablelynx.com
501-279-6223
fax 501-279-6218

Woodruff –74
1

Jean Carter
P. O. Box 492
Augusta 72006 . . . .

wcccourt@hotmail.com
870-347-2391
fax 870-347-8703

Yell – 75
15

Sharon S. Barnett
Courthouse
P.O. Box 219
Danville 72833 . . . .

yellclerk@arkansasclerks.com

479-495-4850
fax 479-495-4875

Courthouse
Union Street
Dardanelle 72834 . . . .

479-229-4404
fax 479-229-5634

PROSECUTING ATTORNEYS

(Note: Judicial District map on page 1)

1st Judicial District
    Fletcher Long
    313 S. Izard Street, P.O. Box 365   870-261-1747
    Forrest City 72335. . . . . fax 870-261-1742

2d Judicial District
    Scott Ellington
    Courthouse Annex
    511 Union Street, Suite 342   870-972-4779
    Jonesboro 72401 . . . . fax 870-972-1700

3d Judicial District
    Henry H. Boyce
    Jackson County Courthouse
    208 Main Street, Suite 31   870-523-7428
    Newport 72112.. . . . . fax 870-523-7433

4th Judicial District
    John Threet
    Washington County Court Building
    280 North College, Suite 301   479-444-1570
    Fayetteville 72701. . . . . fax 479-444-1594

5th Judicial District
    David Gibbons
    Pope County Courthouse
    100 W. Main Street, 4th floor   479-968-8600
    Russellville 72801. . . . . fax 479-967-1086

6th Judicial District
    Larry Jegley
    224 South Spring Street   501-340-8000
    Little Rock 72201 . . . . fax 501-340-8049
        Administration. 501-340-8000
        Citizen Complaints. 501-340-8100
        Felony Case Records. 501-340-8098
        Hot Checks. 501-340-8096
        Victim-Witness Assistance. 501-340-8000

District Court offices:

Little Rock. 501-371-4508
North Little Rock. 501-758-5198
Pulaski County. 501-340-6828
Jacksonville. 501-985-2229
Sherwood. 501-833-0630

7th Judicial District
Eddy Easley (must resign effective 12/31/12)
215 E. Highland, Suite 4   870-337-1468
Malvern 72140 . . . . fax 870-337-9441

8N Judicial District
Christi McQueen
P.O. Box 1216   870-777-0900
Hope 71802 . . . . fax 870-722-2904

8S Judicial District
Carlton Jones
412 Laurel Ave., Suite 6   870-774-1002
Texarkana 71854 . . . . fax 870-772-9315

9E Judicial District
Blake Batson
414 Court Street   870-246-9868
Arkadelphia 71923 . . . . fax 888-251-9536

9W Judicial District
Bryan Chesshir
P.O. Box 158   870-845-5030
Ashdown 71852 . . . . fax 870-845-0268

10th Judicial District
Thomas Deen
506 South Main Street   870-367-9896
Monticello 71655 . . . . fax 870-367-9696

11E Judicial District
Robert Dittrich
305 S. College, P.O. Box 845   870-673-3048
Stuttgart 72160 . . . . fax 870-673-4431

11W Judicial District
    Kyle Hunter
    101 West Barraque, P.O. Box 9090   870-541-5387
    Pine Bluff 71611.................................... fax 870-536-3613

12th Judicial District
    Daniel Shue
    901 South B Street, Suite 209   479-783-8976
    Fort Smith 72901 .... fax 479-784-1551

13th Judicial District
    Robin Carroll (must resign 12/31/12)
    307 American Road, Room 114   870-864-1960
    El Dorado 71730 .... fax 870-864-1964

14th Judicial District
    Ron Kincade
    301 East 6th Street, Suite 170   870-425-2595
    Mt. Home 72653 .... fax 870-425-2596

15th Judicial District
    Tom Tatum II
    P.O. Box 1599   479-495-4550
    Dardanelle 72833 .... fax 479-495-7992

16th Judicial District
    Don McSpadden
    368 East Main, Suite 300
    P.O. Box 2051   870-793-8825
    Batesville 72503 .... fax 870-793-8870

17th Judicial District
    Chris Raff
    411 North Spruce   501-279-6236
    Searcy 72143 .... fax 501-279-2072

18E Judicial District
    Steve Oliver
    501 Ouachita Avenue   501-622-3720
    Hot Springs 71901.................................... fax 501-622-3797

18W Judicial District
    Andy Riner
    P.O. Box 1721   479-394-1964
    Mena 71953 . . . . fax 479-394-6173

19E Judicial District
    Tony Rogers
    202 N. Springfield
    P.O. Box 536   479-423-6869
    Berryville 72616 . . . . fax 479-423-6624

19W Judicial District
    Van Stone
    100 Northeast "A" St.   479-271-1030
    Bentonville 72712 . . . . fax 479-271-1076

20th Judicial District
    Cody Hiland
    609 Locust
    P.O. Box 550   501-450-4927
    Conway 72032 . . . . fax 501-450-7607

21st Judicial District
    Marc McCune
    206 South Third Street   479-474-5000
    Van Buren 72956 . . . . fax 479-471-3256

22d Judicial District
    Ken Casady
    Saline County Judicial Bldg.
    102 South Main   501-315-7767
    Benton 72015 . . . . fax 501-315-3171

23d Judicial District
    Chuck Graham
    Courthouse
    301 North Center, Suite 301   501-676-2807
    Lonoke 72086. . . . . fax 501-676-3044

Arkansas State Hospital

Involuntary Commitments Deputy Prosecuting Attorney
Mental Health Court
4710 West Seventh Street (behind and connected to Arkansas State Hospital)
Little Rock 72205.. 501-686-9193

Prosecutor Coordinator

Prosecutor Coordinator's Office
323 Center St., Suite 750   501-682-3671
Little Rock 72201.. fax 501-682-5004

ARKANSAS SUPREME COURT
AND COURT OF APPEALS

Clerk's Office.. 501-682-6849
Criminal Justice Coordinator........................... 501-682-1637
Administrative Office of the Courts.................... 501-682-9400
Language Translators..................................... 501-682-9400
Court Information Services............................... 501-410-1919
Library.. 501-682-2147
Supreme Court Police..................................... 501-682-6068
Committee on Professional Conduct..................... 501-376-0313
Justice Building
625 Marshall St., Little Rock 72201

NOTES

NOTES

ARKANSAS DISTRICT COURTS
2011-2017

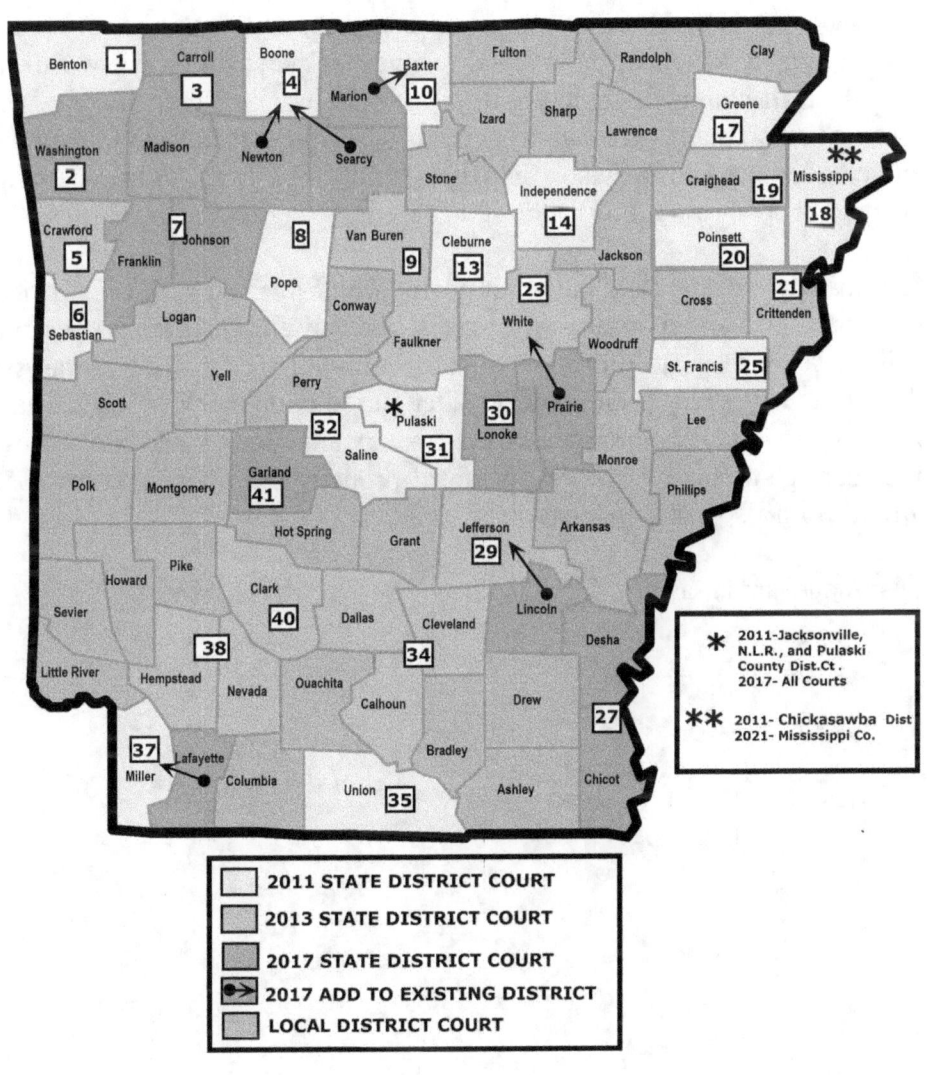

2011-Jacksonville, N.L.R., and Pulaski County Dist.Ct. 2017- All Courts

** 2011- Chickasawba Dist 2021- Mississippi Co.

2011 STATE DISTRICT COURT
2013 STATE DISTRICT COURT
2017 STATE DISTRICT COURT
2017 ADD TO EXISTING DISTRICT
LOCAL DISTRICT COURT

NOTES RE DISTRICT COURTS

District courts are the state's courts of limited jurisdiction. There are two types of district courts: (1) State district courts, and (2) Local district courts.

State district courts are served by twenty-five full-time judges in fifteen counties comprising fifteen numerical districts, effective July 27, 2011. Additional state district courts are created in January 2013 and January 2017. State district courts exercise territorial jurisdiction within judicial districts established by the General Assembly that is city, county or district wide. These courts have subject matter jurisdiction over misdemeanors and violations of state law and local ordinances, preliminary felony cases and civil cases involving contracts, damage to personal property and recovery of personal property in matters less than $25,000. A small claims division provides a forum in which citizens represent themselves to resolve contracts and personal property matters of less than $5,000. Supreme Court Administrative Order Number 18 authorizes state district court judges to hear certain matters filed in circuit court upon referral by the circuit court or the consent of the parties.

The remainders of the state's district courts are designated as local district courts. Local district courts are served by part-time judges who may engage in the private practice of law. Local district courts have territorial jurisdiction as established by the General Assembly, most of which is county wide. Their subject matter jurisdiction includes misdemeanors and violations of state law and local ordinances, preliminary felony cases and civil cases involving contracts, damage to and recovery of personal property in matters less than $5,000. A small claims division also exists in local district courts.

Source: https://courts.arkansas.gov/districtcourt/

DIRECTORY

Notes: (1) City Courts are so marked; all others are District Courts; (2) some courts are in more than one county, so they are listed in all counties; (3) blank addresses after the name mean there is a prior entry in that county's listing; (4) prosecutors for these courts are not included because most are city attorneys but many are deputy prosecuting attorneys and they might vary within the same district.

Department	Judge	Clerk

ARKANSAS COUNTY

Department	Judge	Clerk
DeWitt	B. Park Eldridge, Jr. P.O. Box 35 Gillett 72055 870-548-2672 Fax – 548-2546	Lyn Archambeau 120 Court Square DeWitt 72042 870-946-2503 Fax – 946-1005
Gillett	B. Park Eldridge, Jr.	Jennifer Lowe P.O. Box 367 Gillett 72055 870-548-2541 Fax – 548-3121
St. Charles	B. Park Eldridge, Jr.	Naomi Mitchell P.O. Box 44 St. Charles 72140 870-282-3425 Fax – 282-3777
Stuttgart	J. W. Green, Jr. 304 South Maple Stuttgart 72160 870-673-7363 Fax – 672-9827	Vicky Maxwell 304 South Maple Stuttgart 72160 870-673-7951 Fax – 673-6522 bombayclerk@yahoo.com

ASHLEY COUNTY

Crossett

Billy Hubbell
P.O. Box 574
Crossett 71635
870-364-6114
Fax – 364-6115

Tami Jordan
P.O. Box 459
Crossett 71635
870-364-7620
Fax – 364-6144
tamibaysjordan@yahoo.com

Hamburg

Reid Harrod
P.O. Box 310
Hamburg 71646
870-853-5236
Fax – 853-5237

Norma Hales
P. O. Box 72
Hamburg 71646
870-853-8326
Fax – 853-5433

BAXTER COUNTY

Briarcliff

Van Gearhart
301 E. Sixth St. #130
Mtn. Home 72653
870-425-3140
Fax – 425-9290

Denise Corbin
945 Scenic Drive
Briarcliff 72653
870-491-5762
Fax – 491-5772

Cotter

Van Gearhart

Kay Laughry
P.O. Box 9
Cotter 72626
870-435-6326
Fax – 435-2438

Gassville

Van Gearhart

Christine Johnson
P.O. Box 28
Gassville 72635
870-435-6439
Fax – 425-6276
chrisj@suddenlink.net

Mountain Home

Van Gearhart

Kim Vinson
301 E. Sixth St. #130
Mtn. Home 72653
870-425-3140
Fax – 425-9290

Norfolk	Van Gearhart	Chrissy McFall
		P.O. Box 239
		Norfolk 72658
		870-499-5225
		Fax – 499-5224
		Chrissymcfall@yahoo.com

Salesville	Van Gearhart	Sherl Jacobs
		46 Gillispie Street
		Salesville 72653
		870-499-5675
		Fax – 499-3035

BENTON COUNTY

West	Jeff Conner	Peggy Gunter
	P.O. Box 459	P.O. Box 459
	Gentry 72734	Gentry 72734
	479-736-8579	479-736-8579
	Fax – 736-2140	Fax – 736-2140
		Peggy.dcbew@cox-internet.com

Centerton	Jeff Conner	Elizabeth Hulse
		P.O. Box 100
		Centerton 72719
		479-795-4431
		Fax – 795-2545
		centertoncourt@cox.internet.com

Gravette	Jeff Conner	Peggy Gunter
		604 1st Ave. SE
		Gravett 72736
		479-787-8579
		Fax – 787-2140
		peggy.dcbew@cox-internet.com

Little Flock	Jeff Conner	Grace Fielding
		1500 Little Flock Dr.
		Rogers 72756
		479-636-2081
		Fax – 636-2318

Lowell	Jeff Conner	Johnna Ritche 216 N. Lincoln Lowell 72745 479-770-0166 ext 344 Fax – 659-0894 jritchie@lowellarkansas.gov
Sulphur Springs	Jeff Conner	Peggy Gunter P.O. Box 145 Sulphur Springs 72768 479-298-3103 Fax – 298-3515
Bethel Heights	Stephen Thomas 114 S. Broadway Siloam Springs 72761 479-524-6605 Fax – 524-6915	Amanda Fenton 530 Sunrise Drive Bethel Heights 72764 479-751-7481 Fax – 750-1698
Bentonville	John Skaggs P.O. Box 327 Bentonville 72712 479-271-3328 Fax – 271-3134	Jennifer Lopez-Jones 2706 S. Walton Blvd Bentonville 72712 479-271-3120 Fax – 271-3134 jnichols@bentonvillear.com
Cave Springs	John Skaggs	Thekla Wallis P.O. Box 36 Cave Springs 72718 479-248-1040 twallis@cavespringar.com
Pea Ridge	John Skaggs	Sandy Easley Button P.O. Box 10 Pea Ridge 72751 479-451-1101 Fax – 451-1681 sandye2725@yahoo.com

Rogers	Brad Karren 1901 S. Dixieland Rogers 72758 479-621-1132 Fax – 621-1136	Connie Watson 1901 S. Dixieland Rogers 72758 479-621-1132 Fax – 621-1136 cwatson@rogersark.org
Siloam Springs	Stephen Thomas	Sandy Luetjen P.O. Box 80 Siloam Springs 72761 479-524-4947 Fax – 238-0995

BOONE COUNTY

Alpina	Fred Kirkpatrick P.O. Box 968 Harrison 72601 870-741-2788 Fax – 741-4329	Phyllis McNair P.O. Box 500 Alpena 72611 870-437-2272 Fax – 437-5437 pmcnair@eritter.net
Harrison	Fred Kirkpatrick	Sandra Wright P.O. Box 968 Harrison 72601 870-741-2788 Fax – 741-4329

BRADLEY COUNTY

Warren	Bruce Anderson P.O. Box 352 Warren 71671 870-226-2567 Fax – 226-2685	Joan Taunton P.O. Box 352 Warren 71671 870-226-2567 Fax – 226-2567

CALHOUN COUNTY

Ronnie A. Phillips
P.O. Box 787
Fordyce 71742
870-352-7105
Fax – 352-3160

Cathy Hopper
P.O. Box 783
Hampton 71744
870-798-2753
Fax – 798-3665
chopper71744@yahoo.com

Dana Wetherbee
P.O. Box 864
Hampton 71744
870-798-2165
Fax – 798-2352

CARROLL COUNTY

Berryville

Scott Jackson
104 Public Square
Berryville 72616
870-423-2285
Fax – 423-3630

Betty Neal
103 S. Spring St.
Berryville 72616
870-423-6247
Fax – 423-7069
bdc@bdc.arcoxmail.com

Green Forest

Scott Jackson

Jeannie Beckwith
P.O. Box 1510
Green Forest 72638
870-438-5866

Western

Marianne McBeth
75 Wall Street
Eureka Springs 72632
479-290-3483
c 479-981-1171
Fax – 253-7134

Linda Wishon
44 South Main
Eureka Springs 72632
479-253-8574
Fax – 253-6967
lwhishon@cityofeurekasprings.org

CHICOT COUNTY

Dermott

Chuck Gibson
P.O. Box 510
Dermott 71638
870-538-3288
Fax – 538-5029

Sonya Mays
112 N. Freeman St.
Dermott 71638
870-538-3476
Fax – 538-5252

Eudora	Laurie A. Bridewell 111 N. Archer Eudora 71640 870-265-3993 Fax – 355-4914	Jennifer Bordelon 111 N. Archer Eudora 71640 870-355-2878 Fax – 355-4914 Jennifer_bordelon@yahoo.com
Lake Village	David Gillison, Jr. P.O. Box 669 Lake Village 71653 870-265-2235 Fax – 265-5668	Deborah Oswalt P.O. Box 832 Lake Village 71653 870-265-3283 Fax – 265-5668 lvdistrictcourt@yahoo.com

CLARK COUNTY

Arkadelphia	Randy Hill 419 Clay Street Arkadelphia 71923 870-246-9552 Fax – 246-1415	Staci Huber P.O. Box 449 Arkadelphia 71923 870-246-9552 Fax – 246-1415 stacihuber@yahoo.com
Amity	Randy Hill	Heather Vaughan 309 W. Thompson St. Amity 71921 870-342-5368 Fax – 342-6284
Caddo Valley	Randy Hill 137 Malvern Road Arkadelphia 71923 870-246-8283 Fax – 246-5729	Elizabeth Garner 137 Malvern Road Arkadelphia 71923 870-246-8283 Fax – 246-5729
Gurdon	Randy Hill 419 Clay Street Arkadelphia 71923 870-246-9552 Fax – 246-1415	Staci Huber

| Sparkman
(also Dallas Co.) | Tom Wynne
308 Main St
870-678-2255
Fordyce 71742 | Rita Fite
110 East Main St.
Sparkman 71763
870-678-2255 |

CLAY COUNTY

Corning	David Copelin P.O. Box 402 Piggott 72454 870-598-5547	Linda Dixon 800 S.W. 2nd Street Corning 72422 870-857-0115 Fax – 857-3271 districtclerk@centurytel.net
Piggott	David Copelin	Linda Dixon 151 S. 2nd Avenue Piggott 72454 870-598-2265 Fax – 857-3271
Rector	David Copelin	Starr Boyd 407 S. Stewart Rector 72461 870-595-9805

CLEBURNE COUNTY

Heber Springs	Mike Irwin P.O. Box 368 Heber Springs 72543 501-362-5806 Fax – 362-8715	Tammy Verser 102 East Main Heber Springs 72543 501-362-6585 Fax – 362-4661
Quitman	Mike Irwin	Sherry Davis P.O. Box 159 Quitman 72131 501-589-3512
Concord	Mike Irwin	Pamela Davis P.O. Box 273 Concord 72523 870-668-3315 Fax – 668-3315

Greers Ferry   Mike Irwin   Judy Triplett
                                                    8739 Edgemont Road
                                                    Greers Ferry 72067
                                                    501-825-7172
                                                    Fax 825-8029
                                                    jtriplett.gfcity@yahoo.com

CLEVELAND COUNTY

Rison   Ronnie A. Phillips   Billie Blanchard
                      P.O. Box 787   P.O. Box 855
                      Fordyce 71742   Rison 71665
                      870-352-7105   870-325-7382
                      Fax – 352-3160   Fax – 325-6152

COLUMBIA COUNTY

Magnolia   Francis 'Lucky' Crumpler   Joyce S. Gagnon
                      216 S. Washington   216 S. Washington
                      Magnolia 71753   Magnolia 71753
                      870-234-7312   870-234-7312
                      Fax – 234-7312   Fax – 234-7312

Waldo   Francis 'Lucky' Crumpler   Ora L. Radford
                                                    P.O. Box 369
                                                    Waldo 71770
                                                    870-693-2198
                                                    Fax – 693-2196

CONWAY COUNTY

Morrilton   Howard C. Yates   Doris Coulter
                      P.O. Box 190   P.O. Box 127
                      Morrilton 72110   Morrilton 72110
                      501-354-1505   501-354-9615
                      Fax – 354-1507   Fax – 354-9633
                                                    dcoulter@conwaycounty.org

Menifee	Howard C. Yates	Willie J. Heaggans P.O. Box 38 Menifee 72107 501-354-9763 Fax – 354-0799
Oppelo	Howard C. Yates	Renee McGhee 8 Municipal Drive Oppelo 72115 501-354-2454 Fax – 354-2454
Plummerville	Howard C. Yates	Doris Coulter P.O. Box 7 Plummerville 72110 501-354-6400 Fax – 354-9122

CRAIGHEAD COUNTY

Jonesboro	Keith Blackman 410 W. Washington Jonesboro 72401 870-933-4584 Fax – 933-4582	Joe Monroe 410 W. Washington Jonesboro 72401 870-933-4508 Fax – 933-4582 jmonroe@craigheadcounty.org
Lake City	Keith Blackman	Terry Powell P.O. Box 537 Lake City 72437 870-237-4142 Fax – 237-8174 terry@craigheadcounty.org

CRAWFORD COUNTY

Van Buren	Steven Peer 1003 Broadway Van Buren 72956 479-474-1671 Fax – 471-5005	Carol Ray 1003 Broadway Van Buren 72956 479-474-1671 Fax – 471-5005 cray@vanburencity.org

Alma	Steven Peer	Betty Shores 804 Fayetteville Ave. Alma 72921 479-632-4170 Fax 479-632-4516
Dyer	Steven Peer	Veronica Robins P.O. Box 149 Dyer 72935 479-997-8557
Mountainburg	Steven Peer	Barbara Smith P.O. Box 433 Mountainburg 72946 479-369-2791
Mulberry (also Franklin Co.)	Steven Peer	Marie Johnson P.O. Box 448 Mulberry 72947 479-997-1321 Fax – 997-1232

CRITTENDEN COUNTY

Earle	Mike Stephenson P.O. Box 830 West Memphis 72301 870-732-9100	Gwen Marlow P.O. Box 213 Earle 72331 870-792-8909 Fax – 792-8477
Edmondson	William P. Rainey	(no information)
Gilmore	Mike Stephenson	Noryce Meadley P.O. Box 253 Gilmore 72339 870-343-2697 Fax – 343-2601
Jericho	Mike Stephenson	P.O. Box 10 Crawfordsville 72327 870-739-4918

Marion	Mike Stephenson	Nyree Moore
		P.O. Box 717
		Marion 72364
		870-739-5411
		Fax – 739-2102
		mdc1@mariondc.com

Turrell	Mike Stephenson	Lasonja Harris
		P.O. Box 249
		Turrell 72384
		870-343-2537
		Fax – 343-8728

West Memphis	William P. Rainey	Terry Griffin
	P.O. Box 766	P.O. Box 766
	West Memphis 72303	West Memphis 72303
	870-739-4446	870-732-7560
	Fax – 739-1478	Fax – 732-7566

CROSS COUNTY

Wynne	Joe Boeckmann	Ramona McAvoy
	P.O. Box 786	205 Mississippi St.
	Wynne 72396	Wynne 72396
	870-238-7977	870-238-9171
	Fax – 238-7978	Fax – 238-3930

Cherry Valley	Joe Boeckmann	Terrie Morris
		P.O. Box 130
		Cherry Valley 72324
		870-588-3366
		Fax – 588-4311

Parkin	Joe Boeckmann	Katrina Bohanon
		P.O. Box 498
		Parkin 72373
		870-755-5491
		Fax – 755-2720

DALLAS COUNTY

Fordyce   Tom Wynne   Sandra Wilson
206 W. 3rd St., 2d Fl   206 W. 3rd St., 2d Fl
Fordyce 71742   Fordyce 71742
870-352-5101   870-352-2332
Fax – 352-8707   Fax – 352-3414
sandrawilson2007@gmail.com

Sparkman   Tom Wynne   Rita Fite
 (also Clark Co.)   P.O. Box 165
110 East Main St.
Sparkman 71763
870-678-2255
Fax – 678-2208

DESHA COUNTY

Dumas   Howard 'Corky' Holthoff   Connie Carman
152 S. Main   149 E. Waterman
Dumas 71639   Dumas 71639
870-382-2444   870-382-6972
Fax – 382-2814   Fax – 382-1106

McGehee   Gibbs Ferguson   Connie Moss
109 W. Oak   P.O. Box 11
McGehee 71654   McGehee 71654
870-222-6660   870-222-3859
Fax – 222-6661   Fax – 222-4859
clerkcmoss@yahoo.com

DREW COUNTY

Monticello   Ken Harper   Yukiko Shepherd
P.O. Box 487   P.O. Box 505
Monticello 71657   Monticello 71657
870-367-6102   870-367-4420
Fax – 367-9224   Fax – 460-9056

FAULKNER COUNTY

Note: there are two departments with Faulkner and Van Buren Counties in one district starting in 2013; Susan Weaver and David Reynolds were elected.

Conway
1st Dept.

Amy Brazil
1315 Main St
Conway 72034
501-327-4457
Fax – 327-2183

Donna Clifton
810 Parkway
Conway 72032
501-450-6112
Fax – 450-6184
donna.clifton@cityofconway.org

Damascus
(also in Van
Buren Co.)

Amy Brazil

Lisa Hurst
P.O. Box 309
Damascus 72039
501-335-7203
Fax – 335-7206

Greenbrier

Amy Brazil

Sarah Watson
P.O. Box 415
Greenbrier 72058
501-679-2422
Fax – 679 6007

Guy

Amy Brazil

Wendy Grimes
P.O. Box 12
Guy 72061
501-679-4585

Mayflower

Amy Brazil

Sheila Caudle
33 Culberson Road
Mayflower 72106
501-470-0948
Fax – 470-0543

Mount Vernon

Amy Brazil

Sherri Beeson
P.O. Box 126
Mt. Vernon 72111
501-849-2323
Fax – 849-2002

Vilonia	Amy Brazil	Sherry Lee
		P.O. Box 188
		Vilonia 72173
		501-796-2534
		Fax – 796-2513

FRANKLIN COUNTY

Charleston	Paul Efurd	Melanie Martin
	P.O. Box 129	P.O. Box 426
	Charleston 72933	Charleston 72933
	479-965-2677	479-965-7455
	Fax – 965-1006	Fax – 965-8890
Ozark	Joe Ramos	Sherry Lowrey
	P.O. Box 403	P.O. Box 403
	Ozark 72949	Ozark 72949
	479-965-7577	479-667-4808
	Fax – 667-4599	Fax – 667-4599
Altus	Joe Ramos	Joyce Hurt
		P.O. Box 403
		Ozark 72949
		479-667-4808
		Fax 479-667-4599

FULTON COUNTY

Salem	Jim Short	Cathy Burke
	P.O. Box 988	P.O. Box 928
	Salem 72576	Salem 72576
	870-895-2986	870-895-4136
	Fax – 895-2987	Fax – 895-4137
		cathyb@centurytel.net
Mammoth Springs	Jim Short	Connie Rogers
		P.O. Box 151
		Mammoth Springs 72554
		870-625-7516
		Fax – 870-625-3602

GARLAND COUNTY

Dept. 1	David B. Switzer 607 Ouachita #150 Hot Springs 71901 501-321-6765 Fax – 321-6764	Vickie Asher 607 Ouachita #150 Hot Springs 71901 501-321-6765 Fax – 321-6764 vasher@cityhs.net
Dept. 2	Ralph Ohm 607 Ouachita #150 Hot Springs 71901 501-321-6765 Fax – 321-6764	Vicky Asher
Mountain Pine	Ralph Ohm	Tambrea Bailey P.O. Box 301 Mountain Pine 71956 501-767-4841 Fax – 760-2936

GRANT COUNTY

J. Larry Allen 201 N. Oak Sheridan 72150 870-942-3195 Fax – 942-7885	Vickie D. Sipes P.O. Box 603 Sheridan 72150 870-942-3464 Fax – 942-8885

GREENE COUNTY

Marmaduke	Dan Stidham 2207 Linwood Dr. Paragould 72450 870-236-7600 Fax – 236-7601	Betty Jackson P.O. Box 208 Marmaduke 72443 870-597-2753 Fax – 597-2754
Paragould	Dan Stidham	Robin Moyer 320 W. Court St., #227 Paragould 72450 870-239-7507 Fax – 239-7506 moyerrd@hotmail.com

HEMPSTEAD COUNTY

Tony Yocom
P.O. Box 991
Hope 71802
870-722-2200
Fax – 722-2205

Sherri Rateliff
P.O. Box 1420
Hope 71802
870-777-2525
Fax – 777-7830
Sherri@hopedistrictcourt.com

HOT SPRING COUNTY

Malvern

Sherry Burnett
410 Locust St.
Malvern 72104
501-332-0088
Fax – 332-0056

Melba Russell
305 Locust, Rm. 201
Malvern 72104
501-332-7604
Fax – 332-3144
mdrussell2614@att.net

Donaldson

Sherry Burnett

Danielle Cannon
P.O. Box 121
Friendship 71942
501-384-2111
Fax – 384-2110

Friendship

Sherry Burnett

Danielle Cannon

Rockport

Sherry Burnett

Rori Myers
P.O. Box 442
Malvern 72104
501-332-8700
Fax – 332-8719

HOWARD COUNTY

Jessica Steele Gunter
219 N. Main St.
Nashville 71852
870-845-4532
Fax – 845-3705

Sherlene Sands
426 N. Main St., Ste. 7
Nashville 71852
870-845-7522
Fax – 845-3705
HowardCo.District@live.com

INDEPENDENCE COUNTY

Batesville

Chaney Taylor
P.O. Box 2721
Batesville 72503
870-793-8817
Fax – 793-8875

Tammy Sterling
549 W. Main
Batesville 72501
870-793-8804
Fax – 793-8875

IZARD COUNTY

Melbourne

David Miller
P.O. Box 337
Melbourne 72556
870-368-4390
Fax – 368-5042

Susan Graham
P.O. Box 337
Melbourne 72556
870-368-4390
Fax – 368-5042

Horseshoe Bend

Davis Miller

Michelle Brabowski
704 W. Commerce St.
Horseshoe Bend 72512
870-670-5113
Fax – 670-4358

JACKSON COUNTY

Newport

Barbara Griffin
615 Third Street
Newport 72112
870-523-6568
Fax – 523-4365

Omega Williams
615 Third Street
Newport 72112
870-523-9555
Fax – 523-4365

Diaz

Barbara Griffin
P.O. Box 601
Newport 72112
870-523-3308

Perry Stegall
P.O. Box 136
Diaz 72043
870-523-8559
Fax –523-9477(call first)

Swifton

Barbara Griffin

Beckie Keton
P.O. Box 129
Swifton 72471
870-485-2607
Fax – 485-2662

Tuckerman   Barbara Griffin   Joyce Hembrey
                                                P.O. Box 1117
                                                Tuckerman 72473
                                                870-349-5313
                                                Fax – 349-5336

JEFFERSON COUNTY

Altheimer   Kim Bridgforth   Jeanetta McClinton
                     P.O. Box 8747   P.O. Box 728
                     Pine Bluff 71611   Altheimer 72004
                     870-541-4646   870-766-8229
                     Fax – 541-4640   Fax 870-766-4875

Humphrey   Kim Bridgforth   Rhonda Walker
                                                Box 128
                                                Humphrey 72073
                                                870-873-4615
                                                Fax – 873-4657

Jefferson Co.   Kim Bridgforth   Debbie Drake
                                                P.O. Box 8747
                                                Pine Bluff 71611
                                                870-541-4646
                                                Fax – 541-4640
                                                ddrake@pbpd.org

Pine Bluff   John Kearney   Veronica Young
                     223 East 3d Ave   223 East 3d Ave
                     Pine Bluff 71601   Pine Bluff 71601
                     870-850-7584   870-850-7584
                     Fax – 850-2440   Fax – 850-2440
                                                youngyears@sbcglobal.net

Redfield   Kim Bridgforth   Alta Day
                                                P.O. Box 304
                                                Redfield 72132
                                                501-397-6111
                                                Fax – 397-2350

Wabbaseka   Kim Bridgforth

White Hall	Kim Bridgforth	Kathryn Funderburg
		P.O. Box 20100
		White Hall 71612
		870-247-1420
		Fax – 247-4870

JOHNSON COUNTY

Clarksville	Len Bradley	Marta Chavez
	210 W. Main St.	P.O. Box 581
	Clarksville 72830	Clarksville 72830
	479-754-6000	479-754-8533
	Fax – 754-6557	Fax – 754-6014
		dcmbc@yahoo.com
Lamar	Len Bradley	Ashley Goodman
		P.O. Box 700
		Lamar 72846
		479-885-3846
		Fax – 885-6171
Coal Hill	Len Bradley	Laura A. Bryant
		P.O. Box 218
		Coal Hill 72832
		479-497-2004
		Fax 497-1000

LAFAYETTE COUNTY

Stamps	Edward Cochran	Carolyn Cole
	P.O. Box 335	110 E. 4th Street
	Stamps 71860	Lewsiville 71845
	870-533-2600	870-921-5555
	Fax – 533-2599	Fax – 921-6666
		discourt@wht.net
Bradley	Edward Cochran	Doshie Graves
		P.O. Box 729
		Bradley 71826
		870-894-3377
		Fax – 894-3388

| Lewisville | Edward Cochran | Carolyn Cole |

LAWRENCE COUNTY

Hoxie	William Larry Hayes	Joyce Roberts
	P.O. Box 623	116 NW 3rd St
	Walnut Ridge 72476	Walnut Ridge 72476
	870-886-1140	870-886-1140
	Fax 886-3905	Fax 886-3905
Walnut Ridge	William Larry Hayes	Joyce Roberts
Black Rock	William Larry Hayes	Debbie Downing

LEE COUNTY

	Robert Donovan	Vickey Thompson
	P.O. Box 389	15 East Chestnut
	Marianna 72360	Marianna 72360
	870-295-3434	870-295-7730
	Fax – 295-3445	Fax – 295-5726
		leecountydistrictcourt@gmail.com

LINCOLN COUNTY

Star City/	Victor Harper	Ashley Muckleroy
City Div.	17 S. Lincoln	P.O. Box 219
	Star City 71667	Star City 71667
	870-628-4118	870-628-4166
	Fax - 628-4120	Fax – 628-4055
		ashleymuck@yahoo.com
Star City/	Victor Harper	Tammy Smith
County Div.		300 S. Drew Street
		Star City 71667
		870-628-4904
		Fax – 628-6442
		districtcour00@centurytel.net

Gould	Victor Harper	Lynn Howell P.O. Box 536 Gould 71643 870-263-4475 Fax – 263-4475 lhowell71643@yahoo.com
Grady	Victor Harper	Deborah Vereen P.O. Box 531 Grady 71644 870-479-3904 Fax – 479-3904

LITTLE RIVER COUNTY

Ashdown	John C. Finley III P.O. Box 405 Ashdown 71822 870-898-3147 Fax – 898-3933	Kristi Lynn Lewis 351 N. 2d St. Ste. 8 Ashdown 71822 870-898-7230 Fax – 898-7262
Winthrop	John C. Finlcy III	Emma Cook P.O. Box 176 Winthrop 71866 870-381-7864 Fax – 381-7300

LOGAN COUNTY

Southern	Betsy Danielson 461 East 5th St. Booneville 72927 479-675-4929	Cherry Hughes 461 East 5th St. Booneville 72927 479-675-4929 Fax – 675-0133
Magazine	Elizabeth Danielson	Vickie Smith P.O. Box 376 Magazine 72943 479-969-8550 Fax – 969-2558

Paris	David Cravens	Paula McCaulley
	24 East Main	County Courthouse
	Paris 72855	Paris 72855
	479-963-3131	479-963-3792
	Fax – 963-6444	Fax – 963-2762

LONOKE COUNTY

Cabot	Joe O'Bryan	Rachel Ellis
	P.O. Box 1192	P.O. Box 1113
	Cabot 72023	Cabot 72023
	501-843-8908	501-843-8908
	Fax – 843-8168	Fax – 843-8168
		debi-454@hotmail.com
Ward	Joe O'Bryan	Elizabeth Reed Glover
		P.O. Box 237
		Ward 72176
		501-605-0339
		Fax – 941-4699
		reednana05@yahoo.com
Carlisle	Joseph V. Svoboda	Fever McElyea
	P.O. Box 554	P.O. Box 49
	Carlisle 72024	Carlisle 72024
	870-552-3436	870-552-3436
	Fax – 552-3577	Fax – 552-3677
		reednana05@yahoo.com
England	Joseph V. Svoboda	Diana Wilkins
		P.O. Box 249
		England 72046
		501-842-3904
		Fax – 842-1936
		dwilkins@cityofengland.org
Lonoke	Teresa Smith	Sunnye Freeby
	P.O. Box 48	107 W. 2nd
	Carlisle 72024	Lonoke 72086
	870-552-1444	501-676-3585
	Fax – 866-593-8306	Fax 676-2500
		Sunnyefreeby111751@yahoo.com

MADISON COUNTY

Orville Clift
P.O. Box 1382
Fayetteville 72702
479-650-6433
Fax – 738-2222

Michelle Bohannon
P.O. Box 549
Huntsville 72740
479-738-2911
Fax – 738-6846
mbohannon@huntsvillear.org

MARION COUNTY

Judith Bearden
P.O. Box 301
Yellville 72687
870-449-6030
Fax – 449-1177

Martha Moore
P.O. Box 301
Yellville 72687
870-449-6030
Fax – 449-1177

Bull Shoals

Judith Bearden

Kimberly Williams
P.O. Box 390
Bull Shoals 72619
870-445-4775
Fax – 445-4948

Flipping

Judith Bearden

Sandy Crisenberry
P.O. Box 40
239 E. Main
Flippin, AR 72634
870-453-8300
Fax – 453-5722

MILLER COUNTY

Miller County

Wren Autrey
100 N. Stateline, #2
Texarkana TX 75501
903-798-3017
Fax – 903-793-3588

Wanda Davis
100 N. Stateline, #2
Texarkana TX 75501
903-798-3017
Fax – 793-3588
wdavis@txkusa.org

Texarkana	Wren Autrey	Debbie Thornell
		2300 East Street
		Texarkana 71854
		870-772-2780
		Fax 870-773-3595

MISSISSIPPI COUNTY

Blytheville	Shannon Langston	Grace Haynie
	121 N. 2d St.	121 N. 2d Street
	Blytheville 72315	Blytheville 72315
	870-763-7513	870-763-7513
	Fax – 762-0433	Fax – 762-0433

Dell	Shannon Langston	Cathy Huddleston
		P.O. Box 206
		Dell 72426
		870-564-2659
		Fax – 564-2811
		townofdell@bscn.com

Gosnell	Shannon Langston	Alvque Henderson
		201 S. Airbase Hwy.
		Gosnell 72315
		870-532-8544
		Fax – 532-5958
		nola3@sbcglobal.net

Leachville	Shannon Langston	Rebecca Clowers
		P.O. Box 67
		Leachville 72438
		870-539-6713
		Fax – 539-2490

Manila	Shannon Langston	Brenda Watson
		P.O. Box 895
		Manila 72442
		870-561-4437
		Fax – 561-4438

Osceola Dist.	Mike Gibson	Melissa Cook
	P.O. Box 686	397 W. Keiser
	Osceola 72370	Osceola 72370
	870-563-3700	870-563-1303
	Fax – 563-3714	Fax – 563-2543
		melissarcook2003@yahoo.com

MONROE COUNTY

Brinkley	John W. Martin	Arrica Brasseur
	P.O. Box 472	City Hall
	Brinkley 72021	233 West Cedar
	870-734-1787	Brinkley 72021
	Fax – 734-2302	870-734-2520
		Fax – 734-3163
		brinkleydistrictcourt@hotmail.com

Clarendon	Robert Serio	Amanda Standridge
	P.O. Box 224	270 Madison St.
	Clarendon 72029	Clarendon 72029
	870-747-3813	870-747-5200
	Fax – 747-3767	Fax – 747-3903

Holly Grove	Robert Serio	Pat McGahee
		P.O. Box 430
		Holly Grove 72069
		870-462-3422
		Fax – 462-3580

MONTGOMERY COUNTY

	William McKimm	Treva Lambert
	P.O. Box 667	105 Hwy 270 E. #2
	Mount Ida 71957	Mount Ida 71957
	870-867-2182	870-867-2221
	Fax – 867-2183	Fax – 867-3695
		TJL101@windstream.net

NEVADA COUNTY

Eugene Hale
P.O. Box 5
Prescott 71857
870-887-5634
Fax – 887-5634

Linda Bell
215 E. 2nd Street
Prescott 71857
870-887-6016
Fax – 887-5795
lindab@iocc.com

NEWTON COUNTY

Tommy Martin
P.O. Box 550
Jasper 72641
870-446-5346
Fax – 446-2234

Kortnie D. House
P.O. Box 550
Jasper 72641
870-446-5335
Fax – 446-2234

OUACHITA COUNTY

Camden

Phil Foster
213 Madison Street
Camden 71701
870-837-8300
Fax – 837-5530

Jamie Lawson
213 Madison Street
Camden 71701
870-836-0331
Fax – 837-5530
camdendistrictcourtclerk@cablelynx.com

East Camden

Dan Ives
3060 Roseman
Camden 71701
870-574-0200
Fax – 574-4036

Tommye Holifield
P.O. Box 3046
East Camden 71701
870-574-2900
Fax – 574-2905

Bearden

Dan Ives

Gale Vaughn
P.O. Box 134
Bearden 71720
870-687-2204
Fax – 687-3555

Chidester

Dan Ives

Jeanette Ponder
P.O. Box 26
Chidester 71726
870-685-2906
Fax – 685-2876

Stephens	Dan Ives	Margie L. Wagnon P.O. Box 572 Stephens 71764 870-786-5818 Fax – 836-4265

PERRY COUNTY

	Elizabeth Wise 29 Johnson Loop Perryville 72126 501-333-1204 Fax – 333-1239	Barbara Gipson P.O. Box 186 Perryville 72126 501-889-5296 Fax – 889-5835

PHILLIPS COUNTY

Dept. 1	Durwood King P.O. Box 248 Helena 72342 870-871-7450 Fax – 338-9832	Linda Danley P.O. Box 248 Helena 72342 870-871-7450 Fax – 338-9832 lmdanley@hotmail.com
Dept. 2	J. R. "Rusty" Porter P.O. Box 2747 West Helena 72390 870-572-3751 Fax – 572-3752	Linda Danley
Elaine	Durwood King	Tina Griffith P.O. Box 605 Elaine 72333 870-827-3760 Fax – 827-3377
Lakeview	J.R. "Rusty" Porter	Everlene Tucker 14264 Hwy. 44 Helena 72342 870-827-6341 Fax – 827-6357

| Marvell | J.R. "Rusty" Porter | Tonya Sweatt
P.O. Box 837
Marvell 72366
870-829-2573
Fax – 829-2187 |

PIKE COUNTY

| Murfreesboro | Dana Stone
P.O. Box 197
Murfreesboro 71958
870-887-8065
Fax – 285-3540 | Patricia Robbins
P.O. Box 197
Murfreesboro 71958
870-285-3865
Fax – 285-3540
pikeco.dc@g-mail.com |
| Glenwood | Dana Stone | Brenda Wilson
210 North 2d Street
Glenwood 71943
870-356-3613
Fax – 356-3034 |

POINSETT COUNTY

Harrisburg	Ron Hunter 202 N. East Street Harrisburg 72432 870-578-4110 Fax – 578-4123	Holly Henderson 202 N. East Street Harrisburg 72432 870-578-4110 Fax – 578-4123 michelleroberts@hotmail.com
Lepanto	Ron Hunter	Diane Taylor Ivy P.O. Box 610 Lepanto 72354 870-475-2415 Fax – 475-3161
Marked Tree	Ron Hunter	Ann Tarlton #1 Elm Street Marked Tree 72365 870-358-2024 Fax – 358-7867

Truman	Ron Hunter	Pam Daniel 221 S. Melton Ave. Trumann 72472 870-483-7771 Fax – 483-2620 pgdaniel1999@yahoo.com
Tyronza	Ron Hunter	Donna D. Wood P.O. Box 275 Tyronza 72386 870-487-2168 Fax – 487-2729 cityoftyronza@ritternet.com
Weiner	Ron Hunter	Myra Schwarz 123 West Second Street Weiner 72479 870-684-2284 Fax – 684-7649

POLK COUNTY

Jerry Ryan
509 Hickory Ave
Mena 71953
479-394-3532
Fax – 394-2948

Dena Ross
507 Church Ave.
Mena 71953
479-394-8140
Fax – 394-6199
denaross@yahoo.com

POPE COUNTY

Atkins	Don Bourne 210 N. Shamrock Russellville 72802 479-968-1393 Fax – 968-8050	Crystal Thacker 305 E. Main Street Atkins 72823 479-641-1811 Fax – 641-7052
Dover	Don Bourne	Wilma Lovelady P.O. Box 258 Dover 72837 479-331-4238 Fax – 331-3388

London	Don Bourne	Deby Sorrells P.O. Box 130 London 72847 479-293-4115 Fax – 293-4127
Pottsville	Don Bourne	Jeff Fryer 173 E. Ash Street Pottsville 72858 479-968-3029 Fax – 890-3570 ptsvlcty@csw.com
Russellville	Don Bourne 1506 East 2nd Street Russelville 72801 Fax 968-4166	Judy DuVall 210 N. Shamrock Russellville 72802 479-968-1393 Fax – 968-8050 judy.duvall@russellvillearkansas.org

PRAIRIE COUNTY

Northern	Robert Abney P.O. Box 246 Des Arc 72040 870-256-4183 Fax – 256-4184	Tammy Rogers P.O. Box 389 Des Arc 72040 870-256-3011 Fax – 256-4612
Biscoe	Jim Rhodes III 7958 Rhodes Lane DeValls Bluff 72041 501-998-2225 Fax – 998-2004	Carolyn Prince P.O. Box 187 Biscoe 72017 870-998-2226 Fax - 998-2449 (call first)
DeValls Bluff	Jim Rhodes III	Leah Woodall P.O. Box 297 DeValls Bluff 72041 870-998-2301 Fax – 998-7252

Hazen	Jim Rhodes III	Annette Felts
		P.O. Box 564
		Hazen 72064
		870-255-4514
		Fax – 255-3637
		hazendistrictcourt@cityofhazen.org

PULASKI COUNTY

Jacksonville Dist. Ct.	Robert Batton	Donna Brimmage
	1414 W. Main	1414 W. Main
	Jacksonville 72076	Jacksonville 72076
	501-982-9531	501-982-9531
	Fax – 985-1100	Fax – 985-1100
		dbrimmage@cityofjacksonville.net

Little Rock Dist. Ct.

Dept. 1 Criminal	Alice Lightle	Beverly Kidd
	600 W. Markham	600 W. Markham
	Little Rock 72201	Little Rock 72201
	501-371-4739	501-371-4739
	Fax – 371-4515	Fax – 371-4515

Dept. 2 Traffic	Vic Fleming	Ken Harris
	600 W. Markham	600 W. Markham
	Little Rock 72201	Little Rock 72201
	501-371-4733	501-371-4733
	Fax – 371-4448	Fax – 371-4448
		kharris@littlerock.org

Dept. 3 Environmental & Civil	Mark D. Leverett	Amanda Robinson
	500 W. Markham	500 W. Markham, #112
	Little Rock 72201	Little Rock 72201
	501-371-4454	501-371-4454
		arobinson@littlerock.org

Maumelle Dist. Ct.	Roger Harrod	Michelle Daniel
	100 Millwood Cir.	100 Millwood Cir.
	Maumelle 72113	Maumelle 72113
	501-851-7800	501-851-7800
	Fax – 851-7427	Fax – 851-7427

North Little Rock Dist. Ct., Dept. 1	Jim Hamilton 200 W. Pershing N. Little Rock 72114 501-791-8559 Fax – 791-8599	Vicki Weed 200 W. Pershing N. Little Rock 72114 501-791-8559 Fax – 791-8599 Vicki.weed@nlrpolice.org
Dept. 2	Randy Morley 200 W. Pershing Blvd N. Little Rock 72114 501-791-8562 Fax – 791-8676	Judy West 200 W. Pershing Blvd. N. Little Rock 72114 501-791-8562 Fax – 791-8676 judy.west@nlrpolice.org
Pulaski Co. Dist. Ct.	Wayne Gruber 3001 W. Roosevelt Little Rock 72204 501-340-6832 Fax – 340-6899	Carol Wilkins 3001 W. Roosevelt Little Rock 72204 501-340-6824 Fax – 340-6899
Sherwood Dist. Ct.	Milas "Butch" Hale 4801 N. Hills #1150 N. Little Rock 72116 501-753-4800 Fax – 825-8918	Barbara Collier P.O. Box 6256 Sherwood 72124 501-835-5319 Fax – 835-8918
Wrightsville Dist. Ct.	Rita F. Bailey P.O. Box 237 Wrightsville 72183 501-897-4547 Fax – 897-5647	Sherry Casey P.O. Box 237 Wrightsville 72183 501-897-4547 Fax – 897-5647

RANDOLPH COUNTY

Pocahontas	John Throesch 1510 Pace Road Pocahontas 72455 870-892-9677 Fax – 892-4392	Phyllis Jones 1510 Pace Road Pocahontas 72455 870-942-4033 Fax – 892-4392 districtcourt@suddenlink.com

ST. FRANCIS COUNTY

Forrest City	Stephen Routon	Helen Rhodes
	615 East Cross	615 East Cross
	Forrest City 72335	Forrest City 72335
	870-261-1410	870-261-1410
	Fax – 261-1411	Fax – 261-1411
		SFCCourt@cableynex.com

Hughes	Stephen Routon	None

Madison	Stephen Routon	Ernestine Broadway
		P.O. Box 109
		Madison 72359
		870-633-2172
		Fax – 630-0935

Palestine	Stephen Routon	Christie Gustavus
		P.O. Box 124
		Palestine 72372
		870-581-2489
		Fax – 581-4434

Widener	Stephen Routon	None

SALINE COUNTY

Alexander	Curtis Rickard	Stacy Cyz
	208 South West Third	P.O. Box 610
	Bryant 72022	Alexander 72002
	501-847-5223	501-455-2585
	Fax – 847-1154	Fax – 455-5531

Bauxite	Curtis Rickard	Lindie Landers
		6055 Stanley Circle
		Bauxite 72011
		501-557-5184
		Fax – 557-5291
		llanders@bauxitearkansas.us

Benton	Mike Robinson	Cheryl Spade
	1605 Edison Ave.	1605 Edison Ave.
	Benton 72015	Benton 72015
	501-303-5670	501-303-5670
	Fax – 303-5696	Fax – 303-5696
		cherylspade@sbcglobal.net
Bryant	Curtis Rickard	Lindsey Dinwiddie
		208 South West 3rd
		Bryant 72022
		501-847-5223
		Fax – 847-1154
		ldinwiddie@sbcglobal.net
Haskell	Curtis Rickard	Brenda Mashburn
		2520 Hwy 229
		Haskell 72015
		501-776-2666
		Fax – 776-1201
		courtclerk@cityofhaskell.org
Shannon Hills	Curtis Rickard	Stacey Cook
		10401 High Road East
		Shannon Hills 72103
		501-455-2003
		Fax – 455-3103
		eyeofmine@aol.com

SCOTT COUNTY

Waldron	Donald Goodner	Jean Billings
	P.O. Box 567	100 East First, Box 15
	Waldron 72958	Waldron 72958
	479-637-3286	479-637-4694
	Fax – 637-4062	Fax – 637-4199
		scdcjean@yahoo.com

SEARCY COUNTY

Marshall

Mitch Cash
P.O. Box 247
Marshall 72650
870-448-3600
Fax – 448-5692

Sandi Horton
P.O. Box 885
Marshall 72650
870-448-5411
Fax – 448-5692

SEBASTIAN COUNTY

Fort Smith
Dept. 1

Ben Beland
Sebastian Cty.Crts.B
901 South "B" St.
Fort Smith 72901
479-784-2427
Fax – 784-2438

Rachel J. Sims
Sebastian Cty. Crts.B.
901 South "B" St.
Fort Smith 72901
479-784-2440
Fax – 784-2438
rsims@fortsmith.ar.gov

Dept. 2

David P. Saxon
Sebastian Cty Crts.Bldg.
901 South "B" St.
Fort Smith 72901
479-784-2429
Fax – 784-2438

Rachel J. Sims

Dept. 3

Claire L. Borengasser
Sebastian Cty Crts. Bldg.
901 South "B" St.
Fort Smith 72901
479-784-2420

Rachel J. Sims

Barling

Wayland Parker II
P.O. Box 925
Greenwood 72936
479-996-6501
Fax – 996-1175

Cindy DuBois
P.O. Box 23039
Barling 72923
479-452-1550 Ext. 211
Fax – 452-3220
kstcyr@barlingar.com

Central City

Wayland Parker II

Florene Brown
1101 Hwy 255
Central City 72941
479-452-6680

Greenwood   Wayland Parker II   Cheri Mitch
P.O. Box 925
Greenwood 72936
479-996-6501
Fax – 996-1175
cmitch@co.sebastian.ar.us

SEVIER COUNTY

Stephen W. Tedder   Phyllis Price
200 W.Collin Raye 101B   115 N. 3d, Rm 215
DeQueen 71832   DeQueen 71832
870-584-3337   870-584-7311
Fax – 642-6651   Fax – 642-6651

SHARP COUNTY

Ash Flat   Mark R. Johnson   Amanda Brewer
2423A Hwy 62/412   P.O. Box 2
Hardy 72542   Ash Flat 72513
870-856-3211   870-994-2745
Fax – 856-3212   Fax – 994-7109

Cherokee   Mark R. Johnson   Joan Romans
Village   P.O. Box 129
Cherokee Village 72525
870-257-5522
Fax – 257-5524

STONE COUNTY

Whitman W. Fowlkes   Emmie Gentry
P.O. Box 1050   107 W. Main, Suite H
Mountain View 72560   Mountain View 72560
870-269-4533   870-269-3465

UNION COUNTY

George Van Hook, Jr.
3801 Oleta
El Dorado 71730
870-864-1950
Fax – 864-1955

Patricia Johnson
250 American Rd. #A
El Dorado 71730
870-864-1950
Fax – 864-1955

VAN BUREN COUNTY

Clinton

John Aldworth
203 Court Street
Clinton 72031
501-745-8801
Fax – 745-6262

Debbie Gray
108 Boykin St
Clinton 72031
501-745-8894
Fax – 745-5810

WASHINGTON COUNTY

Elkins

Ray Reynolds
28 S. College #3
Fayetteville 72701
479-521-0503
Fax – 521-3867

Rene Allen
1874 Stokenbury Rd.
Elkins 72727
479-643-4170
Fax – 643-3368

Elm Springs

Earnest Cate
201 N. Spring
Springdale 72764
479-450-8563
Fax – 750-8564

Glenda Pettus
P.O. Box 74
Elm Springs 72728
479-248-7323
Fax – 248-1092

Farmington

Graham Nations
P.O. Box 979
Prairie Grove 72753
479-846-3467
Fax – 846-3467

Jimmy Story
P.O. Box 150
Farmington 72730
479-267-3865
Fax – 267-5511

Fayetteville

Rudy Moore
176 S. Church, #1
Fayetteville 72701
479-587-3591
Fax – 444-3480

Dena Stockalper
176 S. Church,, #1
Fayetteville 72701
479-587-3591
Fax – 444-3480
dstockalper@ci.fayetteville.ar.us

Greenland	Casey Jones	Tammy Shaffer
	P.O. Box 339	P.O. Box 67
	West Fork 72774	Greenland 72737
	479-839-3249	479-521-5760
	Fax – 575-8373	Fax – 521-7780
Johnson	Earnes Cate	Betty Whittaker
		P.O. Box 563
		Johnson 72741
		479-521-3192
		Fax – 521-9157
Lincoln	Graham Nations	Tracy Irwin
		P.O. Box 967
		Lincoln 72744
		479-824-3321
		Fax – 824-4126
Prairie Grove	Graham Nations	Susie Copeland
	P.O. Box 979	P.O. Box 329
	Prairie Grove 72753	Prairie Grove 72753
	479-846-1888	479-846-3467
	Fax – 846-1844	Fax – 846-5548
		susiebc@gmail.com
Springdale	Ernest B. Cate	Betty Lee
		201 N. Spring St.
		Springdale 72764
		479-750-8143
		Fax – 750-8564
		blee@springdalear.gov
West Fork	Casey Jones	Pauletta Welch
		P.O. Box 339
		West Fork 72774
		479-839-3249
		Fax – 839-3335
		pauletta@westforkar.gov

WHITE COUNTY

Bald Knob	Mark Pate P.O. Box 958 Searcy 72143 501-268-6900	Joyce Britton P.O. Box 119 Bald Knob 72010 501-724-5701 Fax – 724-2909
Beebe	Teresa Hughes P.O. Box 91 Searcy 72143 501-268-0504 Fax – 268-3208	Judy Chandler 201 West Illinois Beebe 72012 501-882-8110 Fax – 882-8113 whitedcbeebe@hotmail.com
Kensett	Mark Pate	Tracy O'Connor 101 N.E. 1st Street Kensett 72082 501-742-3191 Fax – 742-3297
Searcy	Mark A. Pate	Linda Maddox P.O. Box 958 Searcy 72145 501-268-7622 Fax – 305-4638
Bald Knob	Mark A. Pate	Joyce Dunn P.O. Drawer 1119 Bald Knob 72010 501-724-5701 Fax – 724-2909
Bradford	Mark A. Pate	Mellissa Goad 308 West Walnut Street Bradford 72020 501-344-2252 Fax – 344-2252
McRae	Mark A. Pate	Mary Lynn Claiborne P.O. Box 189 McRae 72102 501-726-3621 Fax – 726-3013

Pangburn	Mark A. Pate	Shirley Ramsey P.O. Box 577 Pangburn 72121 501-728-4611 Fax – 728-4250
Rosebud	Mark A. Pate	Wyevette Jackson P.O. Box 219 Rosebud 72137 501-556-4967 Fax – 556-4209

WOODRUFF COUNTY

Augusta	John D. Eldridge III P.O. Box 479 Augusta 72006 870-347-2521 Fax – 347-5084	Essie Nichols P.O. Box 381 Augusta 72006 870-347-2790 Fax – 347-2436 cityofaugusta@gmail.com
Cotton Plant	John D. Eldridge III	Essie Nichols
McCrory	John D. Eldridge III	Martha Wampler P.O. Box 897 McCrory 72101 870-731-2041 Fax – 731-5159 mwampler01@hotmail.com
Patterson	John D. Eldridge III	Essie Nichols P.O. Box 40 Patterson 72123 870-731-5057

YELL COUNTY

Northern Dist.   Kristin Clerk   Vicki George
1310 W. Main # 101   County Courthouse
Russellville 72801   Dardanelle 72834
479-967-3555   479-229-1389
Fax – 967-3556   Fax – 229-5740

Southern Dist.   Bill Strait   Vicki George
P.O. Box 69
Morrilton 72110
501-477-2296
Fax – 495-5944

U.S. DISTRICT COURTS

EASTERN DISTRICT OF ARKANSAS

http://www.are.uscourts.gov/

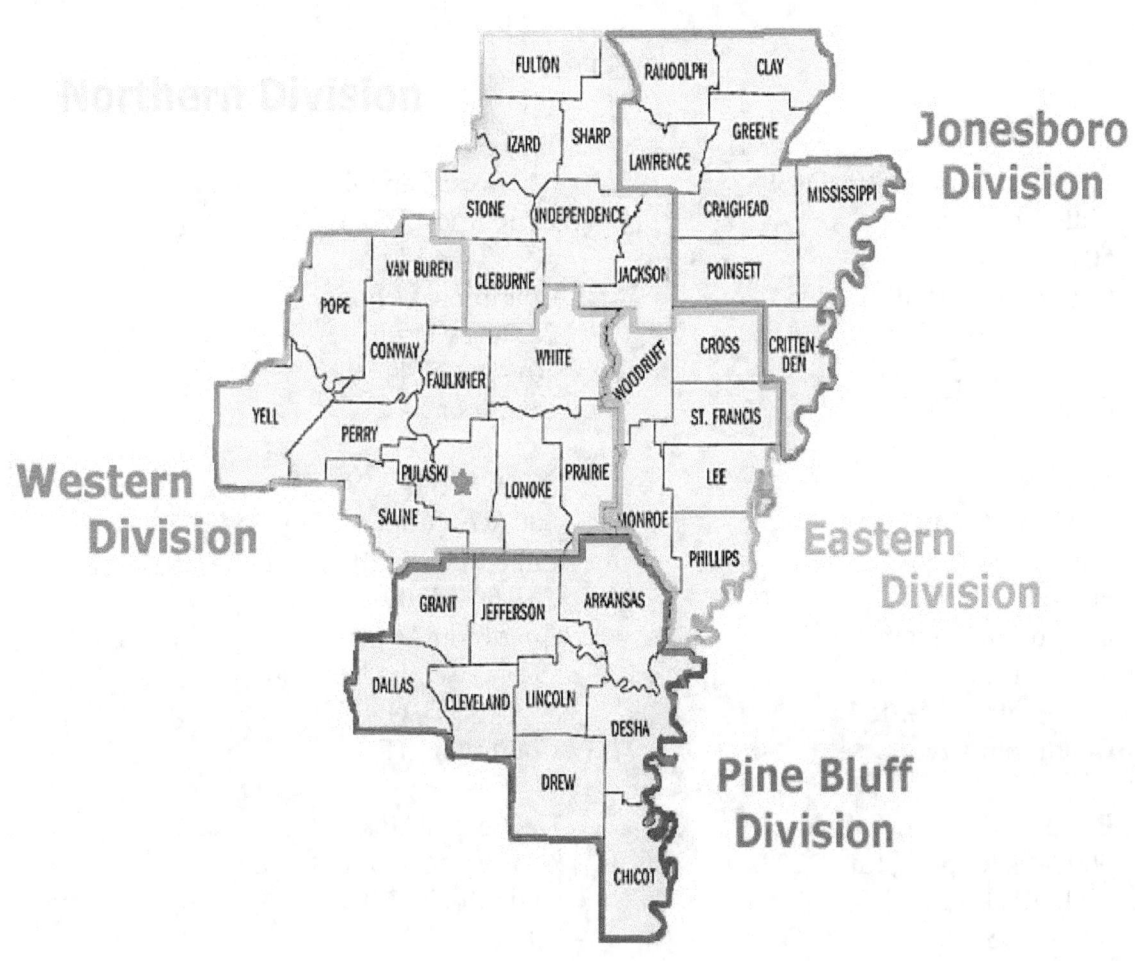

Clerk's Office

U.S. District Court Clerk's Office
James W. McCormack, Clerk
600 W. Capitol Ave., Room A149
Little Rock 72201. 501-604-5351

CM/ECF Support
501-604-5323

Batesville Divisional Office
490 College Street
Batesville 72501
870-793-4330

Helena Divisional Office
617 Walnut
Helena 72342
870-338-6321

Jonesboro Divisional Office
615 South Main, Room 312
Jonesboro 72401
870-972-4610

Pine Bluff Divisional Office
100 E 8th Ave., Room 3103
Pine Bluff 71601
870-536-1190

U.S. DISTRICT JUDGES

J. Leon Holmes
500 West Capitol, Rm. D469
Little Rock 72201
501-604-5380
Courtroom Deputy:
    Cory Wilkins
      501-604-5384
Courtroom: 4D

William R. Wilson, Jr.
500 West Capitol, Rm. A403
Little Rock 72201
501-604-5140
Courtroom Deputy:
    Patricia Murray
    501-604-5144
Courtroom: 4C

James M. Moody
500 West Capitol, Rm. C446
Little Rock 72201
501-604-5150
Courtroom Deputy:
    Donna Jackson
      501-604-5154
Courtroom: 4A

Susan Webber Wright
600 West Capitol, Rm. A522
Little Rock 72201
501-604-5100
Courtroom Deputy:
      Cecilia Norwood
      501-604-5104
Courtroom: 1D

Brian S. Miller, Chief Judge
500 West Capitol, Rm. D258
Little Rock 72201
501-604-5400
Courtroom Deputy:
    Betty Tyree
      501-604-5404
Courtroom: 2D

D. P. Marshall Jr.
600 West Capitol, Rm. B155
Little Rock 72201
501-604-5410
Courtroom Deputy:
      Martha Fugate
      501-604-5410
Courtroom: 155

Kristine G. Baker
500 West Capitol; Rm. C444
Little Rock 72201
501-604-5420
Courtroom Deputy:
    Debbie Craft
      501-604-5424
Courtroom: 4C

Retired:
G. Thomas Eisele
500 West Capitol, Rm. C244
Little Rock 72201
501-604-5160

Court Reporters
(not assigned to judges)

Judy Ammons, Room C118, Judy.Ammons@aredcourtreporters.com. 501-604-5165
Karen Baker, Room C118, Karen.Baker@aredcourtreporters.com. 501-604-5125
Elaine Hinson, Room C415, hinson.elaine@gmail.com. 501-604-5155
Cheryl Nelson Keller, Room C118, cbnrealtime@yahoo.com. 501-604-5105
Christa Newburg, Room C415, Christa.Newburg@aredcourtreporters.com. . 501-604-5145
Eugenia Power, Room C415, GeniePower@swbell.net. 501-604-5115
        500 West Capitol
        Little Rock 72201

U.S. Magistrate Judges

Jerry W. Cavaneau
500 West Capitol, Rm. C163
Little Rock 72201
501-604-5200
Courtroom Deputy:
        Shauna Bostic
        501-604-5204
Courtroom: 1B

H. David Young
500 West Capitol, Rm. C255
Little Rock 72201
501-604-5180
Courtroom Deputy:
        Lorna Jones
        501-604-5184
Courtroom: 2B

J. Thomas Ray, Chief USMJ
500 West Capitol, Rm. C150
Little Rock 72201
501-604-5110
Courtroom Deputy:
        Kathy Swanson
        501-604-5234
Courtroom: 1A

Beth Deere
500 West Capitol, Rm. D14
Little Rock 72201
501-604-5230
Courtroom Deputy:
        Suzy Flippen
        501-604-5114
Courtroom: 1C

Joseph J. Volpe
500 West Capitol, Rm. D245
Little Rock 72201
501-604-5190
Courtroom Deputy:
        Jeannie Smith
        501-604-5190
Courtroom: 2C

Jerome T. Kearney
500 West Capitol, Room C459
Little Rock 72201
501-604-5170
Courtroom Deputy:
        LaShawn Coleman
        501-604-5174
Courtroom: 4B

U.S. Probation and Pretrial Services Offices

Main Office
A228 U.S. Courthouse 501-604-5240
600 West Capitol Ave... fax 501-324-5641
Little Rock 72201................................... PSR fax 501-374-3526

321 Federal Building
615 S. Main St., Room 321 870-935-1510
Jonesboro 72401. .... fax 870-935-4977

3113 Federal Building
100 E. 8th St., Room 3113 870-536-4130
Pine Bluff 71601.. fax 870-534-8498

U.S. Marshal
www.usmarshals.gov/district/ar-e/

USM Clifton ("Chip") T. Massanelli
A328 U.S. Courthouse 501-324-6256
600 West Capitol, Little Rock 72201 .... fax 501-324-6252
        CSO Screening Station................................. 501-324-6248

615 South Main, Jonesboro 72401............................. 870-972-4611
                                                           fax 870-972-4690
Not staffed unless court in session:
        490 College Street, Batesville 72501 501-324-6256
        617 Walnut Street, Helena-W. Helena 72342............ 501-324-6256
        100 E. Eighth Street, Pine Bluff 71601............... 501-324-6256

U.S. Attorney's Office
http://www.justice.gov/usao/are/

Christopher R. Thyer
425 West Capitol Ave, Suite 500
P.O. Box 1229 (72203). 501-340-2600
Little Rock 72201.. fax 501-340-2728

WESTERN DISTRICT OF ARKANSAS

http://www.arwd.uscourts.gov/

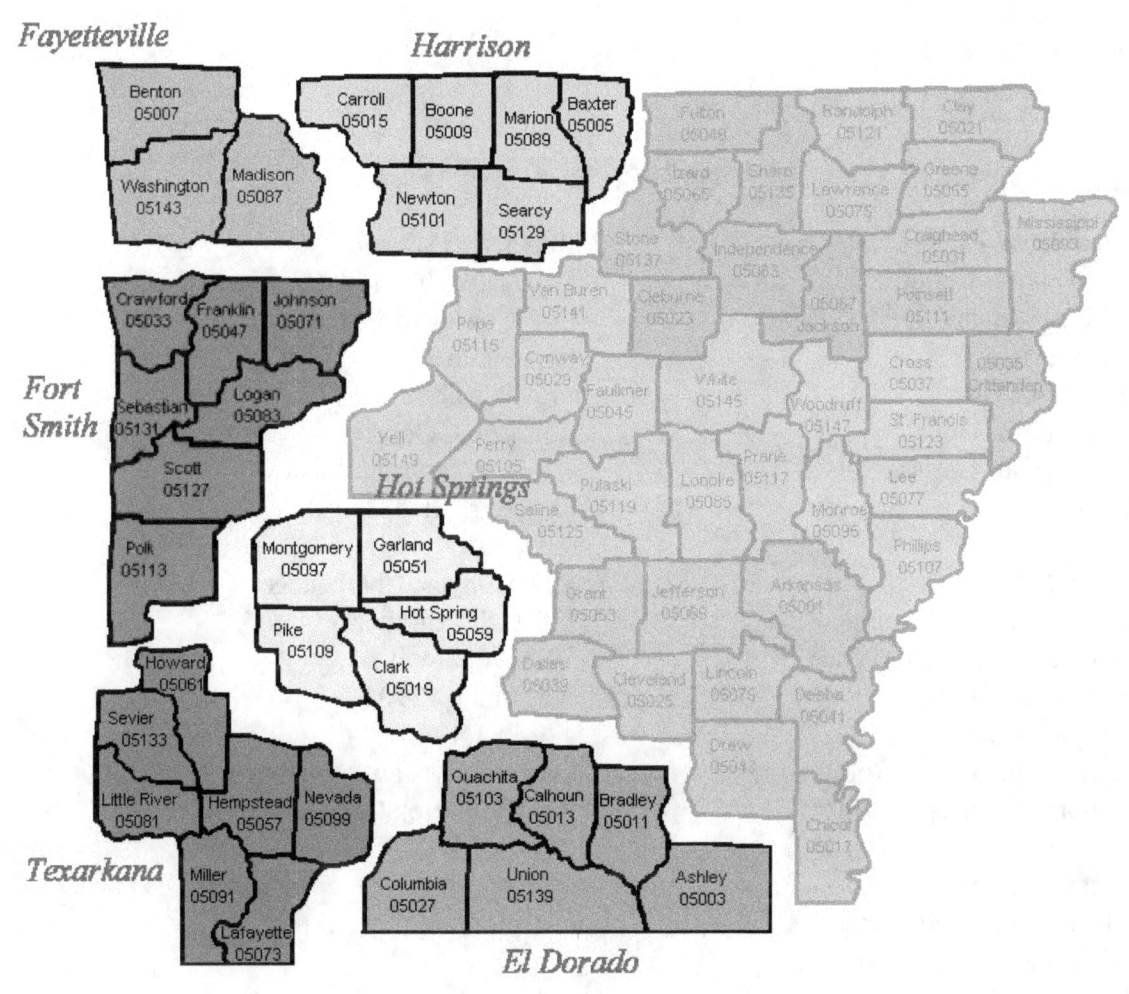

Clerk's Offices

Main Office
30 South 6th St., Room 1038
P.O. Box 1547, 72902
Fort Smith 72901
479-783-6833
fax 479-783-6308

205 U.S. P.O. & Courthouse
101 South Jackson Avenue
El Dorado 71730
870-862-1202
fax 870-863-4880

510 Federal Building
35 East Mountain Street
Fayetteville 72701
479-521-6980
fax 479-575-0774

347 Federal Building (part-time)
100 Reserve Street
Hot Springs 71901
501-623-6411
fax 501-623-8606

302 Federal Building
500 North State Line Ave.
Texarkana 71854
870-773-3381
fax 870-772-4802

U.S. DISTRICT JUDGES

Jimm Larry Hendren
559 Federal Building
35 East Mountain
Fayetteville 72701
479-444-7876
Courtroom Deputy:
    Gail Garner
Reporter: Theresa Sawyer

Harry F. Barnes
210 U.S. P.O. & Courthouse
101 South Jackson Avenue
El Dorado 71730
870-862-1303
Courtroom Deputy: Robin Gray
Reporter: Donna McKinney

Susan O. Hickey
219 U.S. P.O. & Courthouse
101 South Jackson Ave.
El Dorado 71730
870-862-1303
Courtroom Deputy: Robin Gray
Reporter: Donna McKinney

Robert T. Dawson
P. O. Box 1624 (72902)
U.S. Courthouse, 30 S. 6th St.
Fort Smith 72901
479-783-2898
Courtroom Deputy:
    Mokihana Presley
Reporter: Rick Congdon

P.K. Holmes, Chief Judge
317 U.S. Courthouse
30 S. 6th Street
Fort Smith 72901
479-783-1466
Crtrm. Dpty: Jane Ann Short
Reporter: Rick Congdon

U. S. Magistrate Judges

James R. Marschewski
234 U.S. Courthouse
30 S. 6th Street
Fort Smith 72901-2422
479-783-7045
Courtroom Deputy:
     Debbie Maddox

Barry A. Bryant
202 Federal Building
500 N. State Line Ave
Texarkana 71854
870-773-2005
fax 870-773-2014
Courtroom Deputy:
     Danita Gallagher

Erin Setser
213 Federal Building
35 East Mountain
Fayetteville 72701
479-251-1946
Courtroom Deputy:
     Gina Hellums

U.S. Probation Offices

307 U.S. P.O. & Courthouse
101 South Jackson
El Dorado 71730
800-282-5920
870-862-1347

316 Federal Building
35 East Mountain
Fayetteville 72701
800-282-5918
479-442-9892

1063 U.S. Courthouse
30 S. 6th St.
P.O. Box 1564 (72902)
Ft. Smith 71901
800-282-5919
479-783-8050
fax 479-783-5761

308 Federal Building
100 Reserve St
P.O. Box 6199 (71903)
Hot Springs 71902
800-262-5875
501-321-9526
fax 501-321-2689

U.S. Marshal
http://www.usmarshals.gov/district/ar-w/

USM Harold M. Oglesby
243 Federal Building   479-424-5000
30 S. 6th Street, Fort Smith 72901. . . . . fax 479-782-4690

202 U.S. P.O. & Courthouse   870-863-4734
101 S. Jackson, El Dorado 71730. . . . . fax 870-863-7726

516 Federal Building   479-442-6141
35 E. Mountain St., Fayetteville 72701. fax 479-443-1674

352 Federal Building   501-623-9547
100 Reserve St., Hot Springs 71901.. . . . . fax 501-321-9613

500 Stateline Ave. Texarkana 75501. 870-774-9922

U.S. Attorney's Office
http://www.justice.gov/usao/arw/

Connor Eldridge
414 Parker Ave.   479-783-5125
Ft. Smith 72901. . . . . fax 479-783-2442

Texarkana Office. 903-794-9481
Fayetteville (unstaffed).. 479-521-6170
Hot Springs (unstaffed).. 501-620-4229

NOTES

NOTES

Part II:

LAW ENFORCEMENT:
State, County, City, and Federal

See also ACIC Website's
Criminal Justice Directory:
http://www.acic.org/directory/search.php

NOTES

STATE LAW ENFORCEMENT

ARKANSAS STATE POLICE
http://www.asp.state.ar.us/

State Police Headquarters. 501-618-8000
       1 State Police Plaza Drive
       Little Rock 72209

Administration
    Administrative Services. 501-618-8700
    Crimes Against Children. 501-618-8900
    Criminal Investigation. 501-618-8850
    Fire Marshal. 501-618-8624
    Highway Patrol. 501-618-8800
    Public Affairs (PIO). 501-618-8230

Highway Patrol Division Field Offices (Troops)

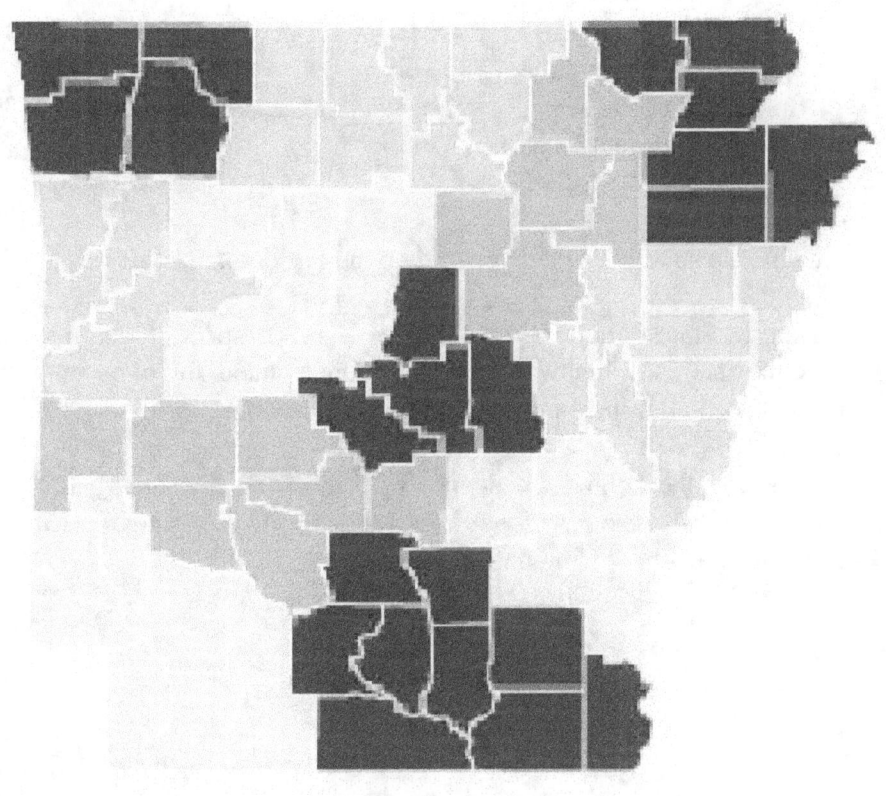

Troop A	Little Rock.	501-618-8282
	1 State Police Plaza, 72209	
Troop B	Newport.	870-523-2701
	3200 Highway 67N, 72112	
Troop C	Jonesboro.	870-935-7302
	2216 Access Rd., 72403	
Troop D	Forrest City..	870-633-1454
	3205 N. Washington, 72335	
Troop E	Pine Bluff.	870-247-1483
	6816 Princeton Pike, 71602	
Troop F	Warren.	870-226-3713
	1237 North Myrtle, 71671	
Troop G	Hope.	870-777-4641
	2501 North Hazel, 71801	
Troop H	Fort Smith.	479-783-5195
	5728 Kelly Highway, 72914	
Troop I	Harrison.	870-741-3455
	2724 Airport Road, 72602	
Troop J	Clarksville.	479-754-3096
	2700 West Main St., 72830	
Troop K	Hot Springs..	501-767-8550
	200 Karen Lane, 71901	
Troop L	Springdale.	479-751-6663
	900 South 48th St., 72762	

ASP Criminal Patrol Unit
        http://www.asp.state.ar.us/divisions/hp/hp_unit_video.html:

        The Arkansas State Police Criminal Patrol Unit is a specialty team assigned
        to work the interstate highways and seek out wanted fugitives and smug-
        glers who may be transporting stolen goods or narcotics.

        Take a look at the behind the scenes operations of this highly successful
        team and see what these Arkansas State Troopers do everyday to stop ship-
        ments of illegal drugs coming into Arkansas.

Criminal Investigation Division Field Offices

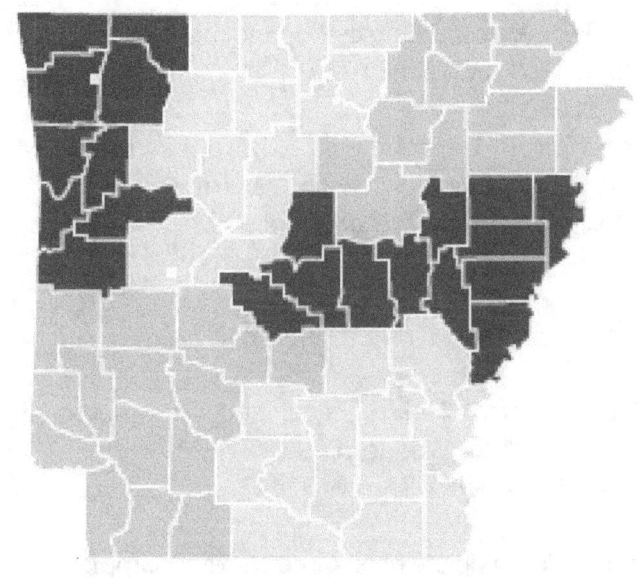

Company A	Little Rock.	501-618-8420
	1 State Police Plaza, 72209	
Company B	Pine Bluff.	870-850-8630
	P.O. Box 8211, 71611	
Company C	Hope.	870-777-8944
	2501 North Hazel, 71801	
Company D	Fort Smith.	479-783-5195
	5728 Kelly Highway, 72914	
Company E	Harrison.	870-741-2136
	2724 Airport Rd., 72602	
Company F	Jonesboro.	870-931-0043
	2216 Access Rd., 72401	

Crimes Against Children – Area Administrators

Area 1 Benton, Madison, Washington
P.O Box 4109, Fort Smith 72914. 479-784-8726

Area 2 Crawford, Franklin, Johnson, Logan, Pope, Sebastian, Yell
P.O. Box 4109, Fort Smith 72914.. 479-783-5194

Area 3 Baxter, Boone, Carroll, Conway, Fulton, Izard, Lawrence, Marion, Newton,
Searcy, Sharp, Randolph, Stone, Van Buren
P.O Box 447, Yellville 72687. 870-449-4058

Area 4 Pulaski
1 State Police Plaza Drive, Little Rock 72209. 501-618-8900

Area 5 Cleburne, Independence, Jackson, Lee, Lonoke, Monroe, Phillips, Prairie,
St. Francis, White, Woodruff
P.O. Box 1210 Heber Springs 72543. 501-206-0343

Area 6 Clay, Craighead, Crittenden, Cross, Greene, Mississippi, Poinsett
809 Goldsmith Rd., P.O. Box 839
Paragould 72451.. 870-236-8723

Area 7 Arkansas, Ashley, Bradley, Calhoun, Chicot, Cleveland, Dallas, Desha,
Drew, Jefferson, Lincoln, Ouachita, Union
Arkansas County DHS
203 S. Leslie St., Stuttgart 72160. 870-673-3597

Area 8 Clark, Columbia, Grant, Hempstead, Hot Spring, Howard, Lafayette, Little
River, Miller, Montgomery, Nevada, Pike, Polk, Scott, Sevier
Sevier County DHS, 304 W. Collin Raye Dr., Suite 108A
DeQueen 71832. 870-642-2623

Area 9 Faulkner, Garland, Perry, Saline
Bryant Police Department
449 Ingram St., Clinton 72022. 870-504-0274

ARKANSAS HIGHWAY POLICE

http://www.arkansashighways.com/highway_
police/highway_police.aspx

Little Rock. 501-569-2421
     10324 Interstate 30
     Little Rock 72209
Alma. 479-474-6074
Ashdown. 870-898-3942
Hope. 870-777-4540
Marion. 870-735-2266
Springdale. 479-756-5831
West Memphis. 870-735-3936
Bridgeport. 870-732-2714
Lehi. 870-735-1162

GAME AND FISH COMMISSION
ENFORCEMENT
http://www.agfc.com/enforcement/

Enforcement Districts:

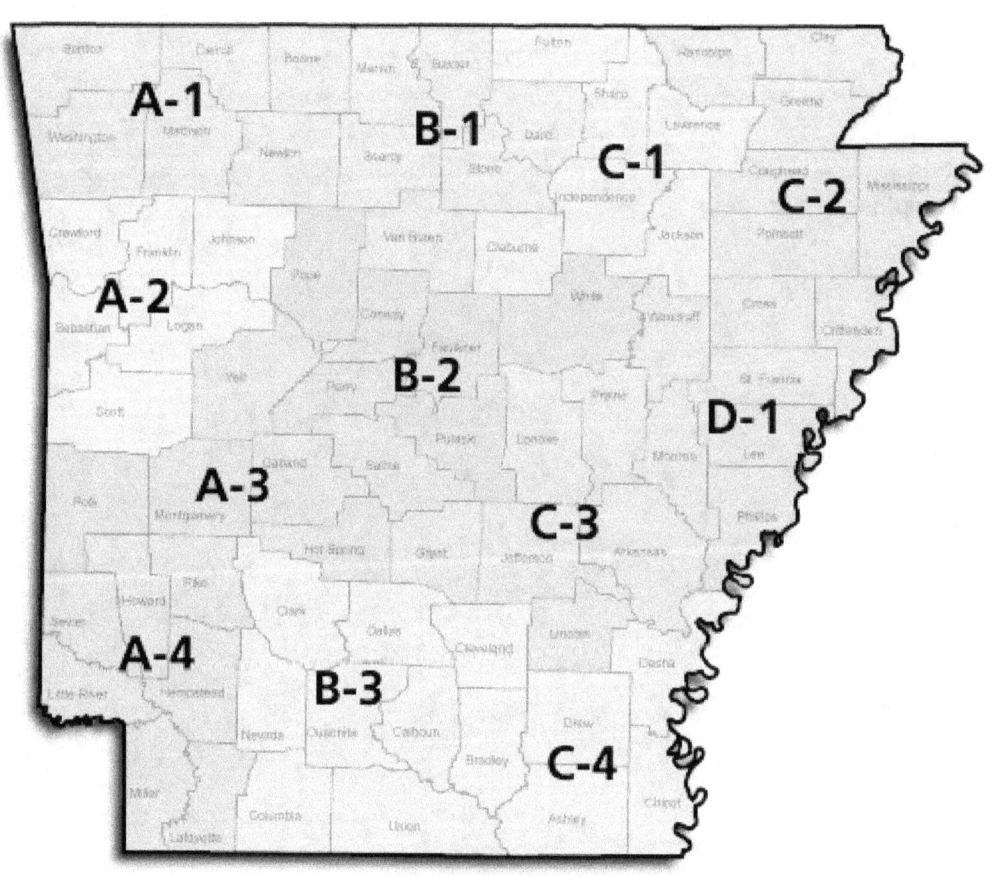

A-1   Benton, Boone, Carroll, Madison, Newton, and Washington
        455 Dam Site Road, Eureka Springs 72631. 866-253-2506

A-2   Crawford, Franklin, Johnson, Logan, Scott, and Sebastian
        8000 Taylor Avenue, Fort Smith 72923. 877-478-1043

A-3   Garland, Hot Spring, Montgomery, Polk, Saline, and Yell
        350 Fish Hatchery Road, Hot Springs 71913. 877-525-8606

A-4   Hempstead, Howard, Lafayette, Little River, Miller, Pike, and Sevier
        P.O. Box 6740, 7004 Hwy. 67 East, Perrytown 71801. 877-777-5580

B-1   Baxter, Izard, Marion, Searcy, Stone, and Van Buren
P.O. Box 729, Hwy. 56 North, Calico Rock 72519. 877-297-4331

B-2   Conway, Faulkner, Perry, Pope, Pulaski, and White
213A Hwy. 89 South, Mayflower 72106. 501-470-1314

B-3   Calhoun, Clark, Columbia, Dallas, Nevada, Ouachita, and Union
P.O. Box 110, 500 Ben Lane, Camden 72701 877-836-4612

C-1   Cleburne, Fulton, Independence, Jackson, Lawrence, and Sharp
895 Hwy. 342, Mammoth Spring 72554. 877-625-7521

C-2   Clay, Craighead, Greene, Mississippi, Poinsett, and Randolph
2920 McClellan Drive, Ste. 1280, Jonesboro 72401. 877-972-5438

C-3   Arkansas, Grant, Jefferson, Lincoln, Lonoke, and Prairie
31 Halowell Lane, Humphrey 72073. 877-873-4651

C-4   Ashley, Bradley, Chicot, Cleveland, Desha, and Drew
771 Jordan, Monticello 71655. 877-367-3559

D-1   Crittenden, Cross, Lee, Monroe, Phillips, St. Francis, and Woodruff
1201 Hwy. 49 North, Brinkley 72021. 877-734-4581

DRUG TASK FORCES

State Drug Director, Fran Flener   frances.flener@arkansas.gov
#1 State Police Plaza Drive   501-618-8690
Little Rock 72209. . . . . fax 501-618-8841

[Notes: (1) The name under the DTF name is the "contract official." (2) The email address may be the supervisor of the DTF, but public records do not always tell. It could be the contract signer. (3) Each has a board of various officials. (4) Some cross judicial district lines although the DTF name does not indicate it, and Texarkana's is bi-state.

1st Judicial District Drug Task Force   drugtaskforce@centurytel.net
Fletcher Long, Prosecuting Attorney
First Judicial District
P.O. Box 365   870-747-5411
Forrest City 72335   fax 870-747-5460
      Area: Cross, Lee, Monroe, Phillips, St. Francis, and Woodruff Cos.
      Board: each county sheriff

2d Judicial District Drug Task Force   ceasterling@jonesboro.org
Scott Ellington, Prosecuting Attorney
Second Judicial District
314 W. Washington, P.O. Box 539   870-932-4355
Jonesboro 72403   fax 870-932-4114
    Area: Clay, Craighead, Greene, Mississippi, Poinsett Cos.
    Board: Prosecuting Attorney, Sheriffs of each county except Poinsett,
        Chiefs of Police of Osceola, Jonesboro, Blytheville

3rd Judicial District Drug Task Force   williams_JC3@yahoo.com
Henry Boyce, Prosecuting Attorney
Third Judicial District Drug Task Force
208 Main Street, Suite 31   870-523-6761
Newport 72112   fax 870-523-7430

4th Judicial District Drug Task Force
City of Fayetteville
Dan Coody, Mayor   kyates@ci.fayetteville.ar.us
City of Fayetteville
100A West Rock Street   479-587-3500
Fayetteville, AR 72701   fax 479-587-3522
    Area: Madison and Washington Cos.
    Board Membership: Chiefs of Police of Fayetteville, Springdale, Prairie
        Grove, and Sheriff of Washington County

5th Judicial District Drug Task Force   DGibbons@popecopa.org
David Gibbons, Prosecuting Attorney
Fifth Judicial District
P.O. Box 1307   479-968-8600
Russellville 72811   fax 479-967-1086
    Area: Franklin, Johnson, Pope Cos.
    Board: Prosecuting Attorney, Sheriffs of each county and Chiefs of Police
        of Russellville, Clarksville, Ozark

Group 6 Narcotics
9th East Judicial District Drug Task Force
Blake Batson, Prosecuting Attorney   blake@clarkcountyprosecutor.com
Ninth East Judicial District   group6@windstream.net
414 Court Street   870-246-9868
Arkadelphia 71923   fax 870-246-8930
    Area: Clark, Hot Spring, Grant Cos.
    Board: Prosecuting Attorneys of 9E and 7, all three sheriffs and Chiefs of
        Police of Arkadelphia, Sheridan, Malvern

South Central Drug Task Force
9th West Judicial District Drug Task Force
Brian Chesshir, Prosecuting Attorney   scdtf1@yahoo.com
Ninth West Judicial District
P.O. Box 985   870-642-8965
DeQueen, AR 71832   fax 870-642-8965
    Area: Hempstead, Howard, Lafayette, Little River, Nevada, Pike, Sevier Cos.
    Board 8S, 9W, 8N Prosecuting Attorneys,   Sheriffs of each county, Chiefs
        of Police of Ashdown, Glenwood, DeQueen, Prescott, Bradley,
        Hope, and Nashville

10th Judicial District Drug Task Force
Thomas Deen, Prosecuting Attorney   mpdnarc1903@yahoo.com
Tenth Judicial District
129 East Jackson; P.O. Box 590   870-460-0900
Monticello, Arkansas 71855   fax 870-460-0221
    Area: Ashley, Bradley, Chicot, Desha, Drew Cos.
    Board: Prosecuting Attorney, Sheriffs of each county and Chiefs of Police
        of Arkansas City, Dermott, Dumas, Eudora, Hamburg, Hermitage,
        Lake Village, McGhee, Monticello, Montrose, Portland, Warren

11th West Judicial District Drug Task Force   Gary.McClain@jeffcoso.com
Stevan Dalrymple, Prosecuting Attorney
Eleventh West Judicial District
117 Main Street   870-540-7466
Pine Bluff 71601   fax 870-541-4618
    Area: Jefferson and Lincoln Cos.
    Board: 11W & 11E Prosecuting Attorneys, Sheriffs of each county, Chief of
        Police of Pine Bluff

12th Judicial District Drug Task Force   dshue@co.sebastian.ar.us
Dan Shue, Prosecuting Attorney
Twelfth Judicial District
901 South "B" Street, Suite 209   479-783-8976
Ft. Smith 72901   fax 479-784-1513
    Area: Crawford and Sebastian Cos.
    Board: 12 & 21 Prosecuting Attorneys, Twelfth District Deputy Prosecuting
        Attorney, 12th Judicial District; Sheriffs of both counties; Chiefs of
        Police, Fort Smith, Greenwood, Barling, Van Buren, Alma Police
        Department; Lieutenant, Arkansas State Police Company H

13th Judicial District Drug Task Force   mikericedea@hotmail.com
Robin Carroll, Prosecuting Attorney
Thirteenth Judicial District
135 Jackson SW   870-836-0906
Camden, AR 71701   fax 870-836-3769
   Area: Calhoun, Cleveland, Columbia, Dallas, Ouachita and Union Cos.
   Board: Each sheriff, Chiefs of Police of Camden, Fordyce, Rison, Magnolia,
     Hampton, Smackover, El Dorado

14th Judicial District Drug Task Force   jpark132@gmail.com
Ronald Kincade, Prosecuting Attorney
Fourteenth Judicial District
P. O. Box 1383   870-425-8454
Harrison 72602   fax 870-741-1874
   Area: Baxter, Boone, Marion, Newton Cos.
   Board: Each of the sheriff, Chiefs of Police of Harrison and Mountain
     Home

15th Judicial District Drug Task Force   ttom@ttatum.com
Tom Tatum II, Prosecuting Attorney
Fifteenth Judicial District Drug Task Force
P.O. Box 1599   479-495-2649
Danville 72833   fax 479-495-7992
   Area: Conway, Logan, Scott, Yell Cos.
   Board: Prosecuting Attorney, Sheriffs of each county, Chiefs of Police,
     Plumerville, Mansfield, Menifee, Paris, Waldron, Plain view,
     Morrilton, Danville, Booneville, Magazine, City of Oppelo (City
     Marshall)

16th Judicial District Drug Task Force   dtml16thpa@yahoo.com
Don McSpadden, Prosecuting Attorney
Sixteenth Judicial District Drug Task Force
368 E. Main St., P. O. Box 4544 (72503)   870-793-8825
Batesville 72501   fax 870-793-8870
   Area: Cleburne, Fulton, Independence, Izard, Stone Cos.
   Board: Prosecuting Attorney, Sheriffs of each county, and Chief of Police of Salem

18th East Judicial District Drug Task Force   soliver@garlandcounty.org
Steve Oliver, Prosecuting Attorney
Eighteenth East Judicial District
501 Ouachita Avenue   501-622-3720
Hot Springs 71901   fax 501-622-3797
   Area: Garland County
   Board: Prosecuting Attorney, Sheriff, Chief of Police of Hot Springs

18th West Judicial District Drug Task Force   twillia735@aol.com
Tim Williamson, Prosecuting Attorney
Eighteenth West Judicial District
141 Elder Street, Suite 2, P.O. Box 1010   479-394-6114
Mount Ida 71957   fax 479-394-6173
       Area: Montgomery and Polk Cos.
       Board: Prosecuting Attorney, both sheriffs

20th Judicial District Drug Task Force   cody.hiland@faulknercounty.org
Cody Hiland, Prosecuting Attorney
Twentieth Judicial District
1403 Robinson Street, P.O. Box 550   501-450-4927
Conway 72034   fax 501-450-7607
       Area: Faulkner, Searcy, Van Buren Cos.
       Board: All sheriffs

Central Arkansas Multi Drug Task Force   blaforce@cityofsearcy.org
City of Searcy, 17th Judicial District Drug Task Force
Belinda LaForce, Mayor
City of Searcy
P. O. Box 178   501-279-1021
Searcy 72143   fax: 501-279-1014
       Area: Lonoke, Prairie, White Cos.
       Board: Chief of Police of Searcy, 17th Judicial District Prosecuting Attorney, Sher-
           iffs of each county, three civilians

Bi-State Drug Task Force
City of Texarkana, Arkansas
Harold Boldt, City Manager   endsley@txkusa.org
City of Texarkana
100 N. State line, P. O. Box 1885   903-798-3130
Texarkana 71854   fax 903-798-3409
       Area: Miller County, Arkansas and Bowie County, Texas
       Board: District Attorney Bowie County, Texas, Sheriffs of both Counties;
           Chiefs of Police and Lieutenants of both cities

OTHER LAW ENFORCEMENT
AND RELATED AGENCIES

ARKANSAS STATE CRIME LABORATORY
http://www.crimelab.arkansas.gov/

Kermit Channell, Director
3 Natural Resources Drive, P.O. Box 8500 (72215)   501-227-5747
Little Rock 72205. . . . . fax 501-227-5936

Dr. Charles Kokes, Medical Examiner. 501-227-5963
                                                                   fax 501-221-1653
Division, Chief
     CoDIS, Mary Robnett. 501-683-6215
     Digital Evidence, Jeff Taylor. 501-683-6237
     DNA, Melissa Myhand 501-683-6220
     Drug Chemist, Gary Dallas, ... 501-683-6187
     Firearms/Toolmarks, Jim Looney 501-683-6170
     Homicide, Eddie Volman. 501-683-6199
     Illicit Labs, Chris Harrison 501-683-6196
     Latent Prints, Bobby Humphries 501-683-6215
     Physical Evidence, Lisa Channell
     Trace 501-683-6183
     Serology. . . . . , 501-683-6261
     Subpoena Coordinators. . . . . 501-683-6152 and -6149
     Toxicologist, Ryan Black 501-683-6213

Hope Regional Laboratory
Jeff Bruce, Chief
2500 S. Main St., P.O. Box 868   870-722-8530
Hope 71801. . . . . fax 870-722-8534

ALCOHOL BEVERAGE CONTROL BOARD

1515 W. Seventh Street
Little Rock 72201
     Administration, Room 503 501-682-1105
     Enforcement, Room 204 501-682-8174

ARKANSAS CRIME INFORMATION CENTER
http://www.acic.org/

Crime Prevention Office
Office of Crime Prevention
Statistical Analysis Center
Uniform Crime Reports Program

One Capitol Mall
Little Rock 72201... 501-682-2222

SEX OFFENDER REGISTRATION
http://www.acic.org/Registration/index.htm

Arkansas Crime Information Center
One Capitol Mall   501-682-2222
Little Rock 72201..................................... fax 501-683-5592

2403 E. Harding Ave., P.O. Box 6209   870-850-8433
Pine Bluff 71611..................................... fax 870-850-8446

STATE CAPITOL POLICE
http://www.sosweb.state.ar.us/

Arkansas State Capitol
Little Rock 72201... 501-682-5173

ARKANSAS SUPREME COURT POLICE
http://www.courts.state.ar.us/

Justice Building
625 Marshall Street
Little Rock 72201... 501-682-6068

UNIVERSITY OF ARKANSAS FOR MEDICAL SCIENCES POLICE
http://www.uams.edu/police/

University of Arkansas for Medical Sciences
        4301 W. Markham, Little Rock 72205....................... 501-686-7777

ARKANSAS SECURITIES DEPARTMENT

Heritage West Building
201 E. Markham, Suite 300   501-324-9260
Little Rock 72201. . . . . fax 501-324-9268

ARKANSAS INSURANCE DEPARTMENT
http://www.insurance.arkansas.gov/

1200 West Third Street   Administration 501-371-2622
Little Rock 72201. . . . . fax 501-371-2629

Criminal Investigation   insurance.fraud@arkansas.gov
1500 West Third Street   501-371-2790
Little Rock 72201   fax 501-371-2799

ARKANSAS STATE PARKS POLICE DEPARTMENT

One Capitol Mall
Little Rock, Arkansas 72201. 501-682-7639

ARKANSAS TOBACCO CONTROL
http://www.arkansas.gov/atcb/index.html

101 East Capitol Ave., Suite 401   501-682-9756
Little Rock 72201. . . . . fax 501-682-9760

Enforcement Agents (regions)
    West, NW . . . . bill.holohan@arkansas.gov
    NW, N Central . . . . glenn.redding@arkansas.gov
    NE, East . . . . james.hickey@arkansas.gov
    East, SE . . . . stacy.m.lewis@arkansas.gov
    W, SW . . . . linda.card@arkansas.gov
    Central . . . . jimmy.massie@arkansas.gov

ARKANSAS RACING COMMISSION

www.dfa.arkansas.gov/offices/racingCommission

Arkansas Racing Division
P.O. Box 3076 (72203)
1515 W. Seventh St., Ste. 505   501-682-1467
Little Rock 72201. . . . . fax 501-682-5273

Thoroughbred Division
P.O. Box 699 (71902)
2705 Central Ave   501-623-1492
Hot Springs 71902. . . . . fax 501-623-9443

Greyhound Division
P.O. Box 2088 (72303)
1550 North Ingram Blvd.   870-732-1331
West Memphis 72301. . . . . fax 870-732-5926

ARKANSAS SCHOLARSHIP LOTTERY

http://myarkansaslottery.com/

124 West Capitol, Suite 1400   501-683-2000
P. O. Box 3238 (72203), Little Rock 72201
Director of Security. 501-683-1896
                                                             fax 501-683-1878

ARKANSAS GOVERNOR'S
LAW ENFORCEMENT AND CORRECTIONS LIAISONS

Arkansas Capitol, Little Rock 72201. 501-682-2345

Liaison to Law Enforcement and Emergency Management
       Larry Robinson. 501-683-6431
Legal Counsel for Clemency and Corrections
       Jenny Wilkinson. 501-683-6447
Staff, Robin Culver. 501-682-8184

ATTORNEY GENERAL'S OFFICE
http://www.ag.arkansas.gov/

323 Center Street, Suite 200
Little Rock 72201

Main number.................................... 501-682-2007
Criminal Department. 501-682-8071
fax 501-682-2083
Medicaid Fraud Department 501-682-7760, 866-810-0016
fax 501-682-8135
Civil Department. 501-682-8077
fax 501-682-2591
Consumer Protection Hotline. 501-682-2341
Racial Profiling Hotline Number. 877-246-4404
1983 Prisoner Litigation Section. 501-682-8077
Director of Security. 501-682-1560

ARKANSAS COMMISSION ON LAW ENFORCEMENT STANDARDS AND TRAINING
http://www.clest.org/

P.O. Box 3106   870-574-1810
East Camden 71711 .... fax 870-574-2706

OFFICE OF LAW ENFORCEMENT STANDARDS

#4 State Police Plaza Drive   501-682-2260
Little Rock 72209............................... fax 501-682-1582

ARKANSAS LAW ENFORCEMENT TRAINING ACADEMY

101 Hussey Road
East Camden 71701. 870-574-1810

LAW ENFORCEMENT PLANNING

Law Enforcement Standards and Training Commission
P. O. Box 3106
East Camden 71701

UNIVERSITY OF ARKANSAS
CRIMINAL JUSTICE INSTITUTE
http://www.cji.edu/

7723 Colonel Glenn Road   501-570-8000, 800-635-6310
Little Rock, Arkansas 72204. . . . . fax 501-565-3081

ARKANSAS CRIME PREVENTION OFFICE

Arkansas Crime Information Center
One Capitol Mall, 4D–200, Little Rock 72201

BJA Strategy Preparation Agency
Department of Finance and Administration
Office of Intergovernmental Services
1515 Building, Suite 417, Little Rock 72201

SENTENCING COMMISSION
http://www.state.ar.us/asc/

101 East Capitol, Suite 470   501-682-5001
Little Rock 72201. . . . . fax 501-682-5018

DEPARTMENT OF EMERGENCY MANAGEMENT
http://www.adem.arkansas.gov/

Director and Central Area Coordinator
Building 9501
Camp Joseph T. Robinson
North Little Rock 72119
501-683-6700

Northwest Area Coordinator
715 West Main, Suite B
Clarksville 72830
479-754-9752

Northeast Area Coordinator
511 Union Room 010
Jonesboro 72401
870-935-3094

Southeast Area Coordinator
210 S. Main Street
Monticello 71655
870-367-3592

Southwest Area Coordinator
2500 S. Main
Hope 71801
870-722-8545

UNION PACIFIC RAILROAD POLICE
http://www.up.com/

UP Police (24/7 emergency nationwide) 888-877-7267
North Little Rock operations main number 501-373-2000

AMTRAK POLICE
http://police.amtrak.com/

Amtrak Police (24/7 emergency nationwide) 800-331-0008

AIRPORTS

POLICE AND
TRANSPORTATION SECURITY
ADMINISTRATION
http://www.tsa.gov/

TSA Contact Center. 866-289-9673
Email: TSA-ContactCenter@dhs.gov

In order of commercial flights, served by TSA:

LITTLE ROCK NATIONAL AIRPORT — LIT
www.fly-lit.com/
One Airport Drive main 501-372-3439
Little Rock 72202 fax 501-372-0612
Little Rock Police 501-374-9004
TSA. 501-212-2001

NORTHWEST ARKANSAS REGIONAL AIRPORT — XNA
www.nwara.com/
One Airport Blvd. main 479-205-1000
Bentonville 72712 fax 479-205-1001
Airport Police 479-205-1020
TSA. 479-254-7815

FORT SMITH REGIONAL AIRPORT — FSM
www.fortsmithairport.com/
6700 McKennon Blvd. 479-452-7000
Fort Smith 72903
Airport Police via FSPD 479-709-5000
TSA. 479-484-8135

TEXARKANA REGIONAL AIRPORT — TXK
www.txkairport.com/
201 Airport Dr.   main 870-774-2171
Texarkana 71854   fax 870-741-5526
Airport Police..870-772-5833
TSA. 870-772-3201

The following are no longer served by TSA, but were in 2010:

HOT SPRINGS MEMORIAL FIELD — HOT
525 Airport Road   501-321-6750
Hot Springs 71913
Airport Police....................................... via HSPD main 501-321-6789

JONESBORO MUNICIPAL AIRPORT — JBR
3901 Lindbergh   870-935-8669
Jonesboro 72403
Airport Police....................................... via JPD main 870-935-5553

BOONE COUNTY REGIONAL AIRPORT — HRO
www.boonecountyairport.com/
2524 Airport Road   870-741-6954
Harrison 72601
Airport Police....................................... via HPD main 870-741-5463

SOUTH ARKANSAS REGIONAL AIRPORT — ELD
www.flyeld.com
418 Airport Dr.   870-881-4192
El Dorado 71730
Airport Police....................................... via EDPD main 870-881-4800

There are about Arkansas 100 airports listed at:
        http://www.airnav.com/airports/us/AR
        http://www.fly.arkansas.gov/AirportInfo.htm

COUNTY AND CITY LAW ENFORCEMENT

SHERIFFS
(showing county and county seat; jails separately listed in Part III)

Arkansas (DeWitt)	870-946-3161
Arkansas (Stuttgart)	870-673-1414
Ashley (Hamburg)	870-853-2040
Baxter (Mountain Home)	870-425-7551
CID	870-425-7637
Benton (Bentonville)	479-271-1008
Boone (Harrison)	870-741-8404
Bradley (Warren)	870-226-3491
Calhoun (Hampton)	870-798-2323
Carroll (Berryville)	870-423-2901
Chicot (Lake Village)	870-265-8020
Clark (Arkadelphia)	870-246-2222
Clay (Piggott)	870-598-2266
Cleburne (Heber Springs)	501-362-8143
Cleveland (Rison)	870-325-6222
Columbia (Magnolia)	870-234-5331
Conway (Morrilton)	501-354-2411
Craighead (Jonesboro)	870-933-4553
Crawford (Van Buren)	479-474-2261
CID	479-474-2581
Crittenden (West Memphis)	870-702-2010
Cross (Wynne)	870-238-5700
Dallas (Fordyce)	870-352-2002
Desha (Arkansas City)	870-877-2327
Drew (Monticello)	870-367-6211
Faulkner (Conway)	501-450-4914
CID	501-450-4917
Franklin (Ozark)	479-667-4127
Fulton (Salem)	870-895-2601
Garland (Hot Springs)	501-622-3660
CID	501-622-3690
Grant (Sheridan)	870-942-5039
Green (Paragould)	870-236-7612
Hempstead (Hope)	870-777-6727
Hot Spring (Malvern)	501-332-3671
Howard (Nashville)	870-845-2626
Independence (Batesville)	870-793-8838
Izard (Melbourne)	870-368-4203

Jackson (Newport). 870-523-5842
Jefferson (Pine Bluff). 870-541-5351
Johnson (Clarksville). 479-754-2200
Lafayette (Lewisville). 870-921-4252
Lawrence (Walnut Ridge).. 870-886-2525
Lee (Marianna). 870-295-7777
Lincoln (Star City). 870-628-4271
Little River (Ashdown). 870-898-5115
Logan (Booneville).. 479-675-3508
Logan (Paris). 479-963-3271
Lonoke (Lonoke).. 501-676-6494
Madison (Huntsville). 479-738-2320
Marion (Yellville). 870-449-4236
Miller (Texarkana). 870-774-3001
Mississippi (Luxora). 870-658-2242
Monroe (Clarendon).. 870-747-3811
Montgomery (Mount Ida). 870-867-3151
Nevada (Prescott).. 870-887-2616
Newton (Jasper). 870-446-5124
Ouachita (Camden).. 870-231-5300
Perry (Perryville). 501-889-2333
Phillips (Helena-West Helena).. 501-889-3309
    CID.. 870-338-5563
Pike (Murfreesboro).. 870-285-3315
Poinsett (Harrisburg). 870-578-5411
Polk (Mena). 479-394-2511
Pope (Russellville).. 479-968-2558
Prairie (Des Arc). 870-256-4137
Pulaski (Little Rock), http://www.pcso.org/. 501-340-6983
    Administration. 501-340-6930
    Investigations. 501-340-6929
    Narcotics. 501-340-6740
    Judicial/Civil Process. 501-340-8450
    Warrants. 501-340-6975
    Substations:
        North East
            323 Roundtop Drive, North Little Rock 72217.. 501-945-8108
                    fax 501-945-1263
        North Central
            25413 Highway 107, Jacksonville 72076.. 501-983-8181
                    fax 501-983-0099
        North West
            10407 Mundo Road, North Little Rock 72118. 501-803-4637
                    fax 501-803-4238

South Central

    10800 Arch Street, Little Rock 72209. 501-888-8990

                                                             fax 501-888-8994

South West

    25724 Kanis Road, Little Rock 72223. 501-821-3976

                                                             fax 501-821-4075

Randolph (Pocahontas)	870-892-8888
St. Francis (Forrest City)	870-633-2611
Saline (Benton)	501-303-5608
Scott (Waldron)	870-637-4155
Searcy (Marshall)	870-448-2340
Sebastian (Fort Smith)	479-783-1051
Sevier (De Queen)	870-642-2125
Sharp (Ash Flat)	870-994-7355
Stone (Mountain View)	870-269-3825
Union (El Dorado)	870-864-1970
Warrants	870-864-1990
Van Buren (Clinton)	501-745-2112
Washington (Fayetteville)	479-444-5700
Warrants	479-444-5800
White (Searcy)	501-279-6279
Woodruff (Augusta)	870-347-5152
Yell (Danville)	479-495-4881
Yell (Dardanelle)	479-229-2533

CITY POLICE DEPARTMENTS

Adona (Perry Co. Sheriff). 501-889-2333
Alexander. 501-455-2585
Alicia (Lawrence Co. Sheriff). 870-886-2525
Allport (Lonoke Co. Sheriff). 501-676-6494
Alma. 479-632-3333
Almyra (Stuttgart Police). 870-673-1414
Alpena (Boone Co. Sheriff). 870-741-8404
Altheimer. 870-766-8665
Altus. 479-468-2286
Amagon (Jackson Co. Sheriff). 870-523-5842
Amity (Clark Co. Sheriff). 870-246-2222
Anthonyville (Crittenden Co. Sheriff). 870-702-2000
Antoine (Pike Co. Sheriff). 870-285-3315
Arkadelphia. 870-246-4545
Arkansas City (Desha Co. Sheriff). 870-877-2327
Ash Flat. 870-994-3061
Ashdown (Little River Co. Sheriff). 870-898-5115
Atkins. 479-641-1811
Aubrey (Lee Co. Sheriff). 870-295-7777
Augusta. 870-347-5189
Austin. 501-843-7856
Avoca (Benton Co. Sheriff) 479-273-5532

Bald Knob. 501-724-5193
Banks (Bradley Co. Sheriff). 870-226-3491
Barling. 479-452-1550
Bassett (Mississippi Co. Sheriff). 870-658-2242
Batesville (Independence Co. Sheriff). 870-793-8838
Bauxite. 501-557-5184
Bay (Craighead Co. Sheriff). 870-933-4550
Bearden. 870-687-3413
Beaver (Carroll Co. Sheriff). 870-423-2901
Beebe. 501-882-3365
Beech Grove (Green Co. Sheriff). 870-236-7612
Beedeville (Jackson Co. Sheriff). 870-523-5842
Bellefonte (Boone Co. Sheriff). 870-741-8404
Belleville (Yell Co. Sheriff). 479-495-2811
Ben Lomond (Sevier Co. Sheriff) 870-642-2125
Benton (www.bentonpolice.org/). 501-778-1171
Bentonville (http://www.bentonvillear.com/police_main.html). 479-273-2455
    Administration. 479-271-3173
    Criminal Investigation. 479-271-3175

Dispatch	479-271-3170
Records	479-271-5890
Bergman (Boone Co. Sheriff)	870-741-8404
Berryville	870-423-3343
Bethel Heights	479-756-3100
Big Flat (Baxter Co. Sheriff)	870-425-2400
Bigelow (Perry Co. Sheriff)	501-889-2333
Biggers (Randolph Co. Sheriff)	870-892-8888
Birdsong (Mississippi Co. Sheriff)	870-658-2242
Biscoe (Prairie Co. Sheriff)	870-256-4137
Bismarck (Hot Spring Co. Sheriff)	501-332-3671
Black Oak (Craighead Co. Sheriff)	870-933-4550
Black Rock (City Hall)	870-878-6792
Black Springs (Montgomery Co. Sheriff)	870-867-3151
Blevins (Hempstead Co. Sheriff)	870-777-6727
Blue Eye (Carroll Co. Sheriff)	870-423-2901
Blue Mountain (Logan Co. Sheriff)	479-963-3271
Bluff City (Nevada Co. Sheriff)	870-887-2616
Blytheville	870-763-4411
Bodcaw (Nevada Co. Sheriff)	870-887-2616
Bonanza (Sebastian Co. Sheriff)	479-783-1051
Bonnerdale (Hot Spring Co. Sheriff)	501-332-3671
Bono (Craighead Co. Sheriff)	870-933-4550
Booneville	479-675-3456
Bradford (City Hall)	501-344-2252
Dradley (City Hall)	870-894-3377
Branch (Franklin Co. Sheriff)	479-667-4127
Briarcliff (Baxter Co. Sheriff)	870-425-2400
Brinkley	870-734-3434
Brookland (Craighead Co. Sheriff)	870-933-4550
Bryant	501-847-0211
Buckner (Lafayette Co. Sheriff)	870-921-4252
Bull Shoals (City Hall)	870-445-4775
Burdette (Mississippi Co. Sheriff)	870-658-2242
Cabot	501-843-6526
Criminal Investigation Division	501-843-6166
Caddo Valley	870-246-6357
Caldwell (St Francis Co. Sheriff)	870-633-2611
Cale (Nevada Co. Sheriff)	870-887-2616
Calico Rock (Izard Co. Sheriff)	870-368-4203
Calion (Union Co. Sheriff)	870-864-1970
Camden	870-836-5755
Cammack Village	501-663-4593

Campbell Station (Jackson Co.)...................................... 870-523-5842
Caraway (Craighead Co. Sheriff)................................... 870-933-4550
Carlisle.. 870-552-3431
Carthage (Dallas Co. Sheriff)...................................... 870-352-2002
Casa (Perry Co. Sheriff)... 501-889-2333
Cash (Craighead Co. Sheriff)....................................... 870-933-4550
Caulksville (Logan Co. Sheriff).................................... 479-963-3271
Cave City.. 870-283-5011
Cave Springs... 479-248-1414
Cedarville (Crawford Co. Sheriff).................................. 479-474-2261
Centerton.. 479-795-4431
Central City (City Hall)... 479-452-6680
Charleston... 479-965-7600
Cherokee Village... 870-257-5225
Cherry Valley.. 870-588-3366
Chester (Crawford Co. Sheriff)..................................... 479-474-2261
Chidester (City Hall).. 870-685-2906
Clarendon.. 870-747-3655
Clarksville.. 479-754-8100
Clinton.. 501-745-4997
Coal Hill (Johnson Co. Sheriff).................................... 479-754-2200
College City (Lawrence Co.).. 870-886-2525
College Station (Pulaski Co. Sheriff).............................. 501-340-6980
Colt (St. Francis Co. Sheriff)..................................... 870-633-2611
Concord.. 870-668-3315
Conway (www.conwaypd.org).. 501-450-6120
    Chief.. 501-450-6126
    Investigative Services Division.............. 501-450-6130
    Narcotics.................................... 501-450-6135
    Office of Professional Responsibility........ 501-450-6126
    Patrol....................................... 501-450-6199
    Records...................................... 501-450-6137
    Warrants..................................... 501-450-6138
Corning.. 870-857-3311
Cotter... 870-435-2122
Cotton Plant... 870-459-3650
Cove (Polk Co. Sheriff).. 479-394-2511
Coy (Lonoke Co. Sheriff)... 501-676-6494
Crawfordsville (Crittenden Co. Sheriff)............................ 870-702-2000
Crossett... 870-364-4131
Cushman.. 870-793-8838

Daisy.. 870-285-3315
Damascus (City Hall)... 501-335-8035

Danville. 479-495-2121
Dardanelle. 479-229-2533
Datto (Clay Co. Sheriff). 870-598-2270
De Valls Bluff.. 870-998-2578
Decatur. 479-752-3911
Delaplaine (Greene Co. Sheriff).. 870-236-7612
Delight (Pike Co. Sheriff).. 870-285-3315
Dell.. 870-838-3008
Denning (Franklin Co. Sheriff). 479-667-4127
DeQueen. 870-642-2213
Dermott.. 870-538-5269
Des Arc. 870-256-3011
De Witt. 870-946-2496
Diamond City. 870-422-7589
Diaz. 870-523-9477
Dierks.. 870-286-2241
Donaldson.. 501-384-2111
Dover (City Hall). 479-331-3270
Dumas.. 870-382-5511
Dyer (Crawford Co. Sheriff). 479-474-2261
Dyess (Mississippi Co. Sheriff). 870-658-2242

Earle (Crittenden Co. Sheriff). 870-702-2000
East Camden (City Hall).. 870-574-2900
East End (Saline Co. Sheriff). 501-303-5642
Edmonson (Crittenden Co. Sheriff).. 870-702-2000
Egypt (Craighead Co. Sheriff). 870-933-4550
Ed Dorado (http://www.eldoradopolice.org/). 870-881-4800
     Administration. 870-881-4822
     Criminal Investigation. 870-881-4810
     Criminal Apprehension Division. 870-881-4802
     Patrol. 870-881-4808
     Special Investigation. 870-881-4830
Elaine. 870-827-3350
Elkins. 479-643-2600
Elm Springs. 479-248-7323
Emerson (Columbia Co. Sheriff). 870-234-5331
Emmett (Nevada Co. Sheriff). 870-887-2616
England.. 501-842-2311
Enola (Faulkner Co. Sheriff). 501-328-5906
Etowah. 870-531-2540
Eudora. 870-355-4412
Eureka Springs. 479-253-8666
Evening Shade (Sharp Co. Sheriff).. 870-994-2211

Everton (Boone Co. Sheriff).. 870-741-8404

Fairfield Bay.. 501-884-6005
Fargo (Monroe Co. Sheriff)... 870-747-3811
Farmington.. 479-267-3411
Fayetteville.. 479-587-3555
    Criminal Investigation... 479-587-3520
    Office of Professional Standards............................... 479-587-3553
    Patrol... 479-587-3555
    Warrants... 479-587-8344
Felsenthal (Union Co. Sheriff).. 870-864-1970
Ferndale (Pulaski Co. Sheriff).. 501-340-6980
Fifty-Six (Stone Co. Sheriff)... 870-269-3825
Fisher (City Hall).. 870-328-7275
Flippin... 870-453-8888
Fordyce... 870-352-2178
Foreman (Marshall's Office)... 870-542-7602
Forrest City.. 870-633-3434
Fort Smith (www.fortsmithpd.org/)....................................... 479-709-5000
    Chief of Police.. 479-709-5143
    Communications... 479-709-5100
    Criminal Investigation... 479-709-5116
    Cyber Investigation Unit....................................... 479-709-5129
    Information... 479-709-5000
    Narcotics Unit... 479-709-5103
    Office of Professional Standards............................... 479-709-5161
    Patrol Supervisor.. 479-709-5012
    Public Information Officer..................................... 479-709-5141
    Warrants... 479-709-5025
Fouke (Miller Co. Sheriff).. 870-774-3001
Fountain Hill (Ashley Co. Sheriff)...................................... 870-853-2040
Fountain Lake (Garland Co. Sheriff)..................................... 501-622-3660
Fourche (Perry Co. Sheriff)... 501-889-2333
Franklin (Izard Co. Sheriff).. 870-368-4203
Friendship.. 501-384-2111
Fulton (Hempstead Co. Sheriff).. 870-777-6727

Garfield (Benton Co. Sheriff)... 479-273-5532
Garland (Miller Co. Sheriff).. 870-774-3001
Garner (White Co. Sheriff).. 501-268-3543
Gassville (City Hall)... 870-435-2615
Gateway (Benton Co. Sheriff).. 479-273-5532
Gentry.. 479-736-8400
Georgetown (White Co. Sheriff).. 501-268-3543

Gilbert (Searcy Co. Sheriff)..................................... 870-448-2340
Gillett (City Hall).. 870-548-2541
Gillham (Sevier Co. Sheriff)..................................... 870-642-2125
Gilmore (Crittenden Co. Sheriff)................................. 870-702-2000
Glenrose (Hot Spring Co. Sheriff)................................ 501-332-3671
Glenwood (City Hall)... 870-356-3333
Goshen (Marshall's Office)....................................... 479-263-7444
Gosnell... 870-532-8545
Gould... 870-263-4907
Grady (City Hall)... 870-479-3904
Grannis... 870-385-7852
Grapevine (Grant Co. Sheriff)................................... 870-942-2101
Gravel Ridge (Pulaski Co. Sheriff).............................. 501-340-6980
Gravette.. 479-787-6948
Green Forest.. 870-438-5517
Greenbrier.. 501-679-3105
Greenland... 479-521-5760
Greenway (Clay Co. Sheriff)..................................... 870-598-2270
Greenwood... 479-996-4119
Greers Ferry (City Hall).. 501-825-7172
Griffithville (White Co. Sheriff)............................... 501-268-3543
Grubbs (Jackson Co. Sheriff).................................... 870-523-5842
Guion (Izard Co. Sheriff)....................................... 870-368-4203
Gurdon.. 870-353-2211
Guy... 501-679-4585

Hackett (City Hall)... 479-638-8107
Hamburg... 870-853-8600
Hampton... 870-798-4610
Hardy... 870-856-2136
Harrell (Calhoun Co. Sheriff)................................... 870-798-2323
Harrisburg.. 870-578-2530
Harrison (www.harrisonpd.org)................................... 870-741-5463
Hartford.. 479-639-2219
Hartman (Johnson Co. Sheriff)................................... 479-754-2200
Haskell... 501-778-4916
Hatfield (Polk Co. Sheriff)..................................... 479-394-2511
Havana (Yell Co. Sheriff)....................................... 479-495-2811
Haynes (Lee Co. Sheriff).. 870-295-7777
Hazen... 870-255-4513
Heber Springs... 501-362-3661
Hector.. 479-284-2533
Helena-West Helena.. 870-572-3441
Hensley (Pulaski Co. Sheriff)................................... 501-340-6980

Hermitage. 870-463-8477
Hickory Plains (Prairie Co. Sheriff). 870-256-4137
Hickory Ridge (Cross Co. Sheriff). 870-238-2365
Higden (Cleburne Co. Sheriff). 501-362-8143
Higginson (White Co. Sheriff). 501-268-3543
Highfill (Benton Co. Sheriff). 479-273-5532
Highland. 870-856-6313
Hindsville (Madison Co. Sheriff). 479-738-2320
Holland (Faulkner Co. Sheriff). 501-328-5906
Holly Grove. 870-462-8008
Hope. 870-777-3434
Horatio (Sevier Co. Sheriff). 870-642-2125
Horseshoe Bend (City Hall). 870-670-5113
Horseshoe Lake (Crittenden Co. Sheriff). 870-702-2000
Hot Springs. 501-321-6789
Hot Springs Village. 501-922-0011
Houston (City Hall). 501-759-2536
Hoxie. 870-886-7701
Hughes (St. Francis Co. Sheriff). 870-633-2611
Humnoke (Lonoke Co. Sheriff). 501-676-6494
Humphrey (Jefferson Co. Sheriff). 870-541-5351
Hunter (Woodruff Co. Sheriff). 870-347-2583
Huntington. 479-928-4023
Huntsville. 479-738-2610
Huttig. 870-943-2233

Imboden (Lawrence Co. Sheriff). 870-886-2525

Jacksonport (Jackson Co. Sheriff). 870-523-5842
Jacksonville. 501-982-3191
Jasper (Newton Co. Sheriff). 870-446-5124
Jennette (Crittenden Co. Sheriff). 870-702-2000
Jerico (Crittenden Co. Sheriff). 870-702-2000
Jerome (Drew Co. Sheriff). 870-367-6211
Johnson. 479-521-3192
Joiner (Mississippi Co. Sheriff). 870-658-2242
Jonesboro. 870-935-5553
Judsonia. 501-729-3454
Junction City. 870-924-5226

Keiser (Mississippi Co. Sheriff). 870-658-2242
Kensett. 501-742-5454
Keo (Lonoke Co. Sheriff). 501-676-6494
Kibler (Crawford Co. Sheriff). 479-474-2261

Kingsland (Cleveland Co. Sheriff)..................................... 870-325-6222
Kirby (Pike Co. Sheriff)... 870-285-3315
Knobel (Clay Co. Sheriff). 870-598-2270
Knoxville (Johnson Co. Sheriff)..................................... 479-754-2200

Lafe (Greene Co. Sheriff)... 870-236-7612
LaGrange (Lee Co. Sheriff). 870-295-7777
Lake City (Craighead Co. Sheriff). 870-933-4550
Lake Hamilton (Garland Co. Sheriff).............................. 501-622-3660
Lake View (Phillips Co. Sheriff). 870-338-5555
Lake Village.. 870-265-5055
Lakeview (Baxter Co. Sheriff)....................................... 870-425-2400
Lamar... 479-885-0405
Langley (Pike Co. Sheriff). 870-285-3315
Lavaca. 479-674-2605
Leachville... 870-539-6713
Lead Hill (Diamond City P.D.).... 870-422-7589
Leola (Grant Co. Sheriff). 870-942-2101
Lepanto... 870-475-2566
Leslie (Searcy Co. Sheriff).. 870-448-2340
Letona (White Co. Sheriff).. 501-268-3543
Lewisville (Lafayette Co. Sheriff). 870-921-4252
Light (Greene Co. Sheriff). 870-236-7612
Lincoln.. 479-824-3351
Little Flock.. 479-936-7911
Little Rock (http://www.littlerock.org/citydepartments/police/)................ 501-371-4605
    Chief of Police.. 501-371-4621
    Airport.. 501-371-9004
    Communications.. 501-371-4540
    Criminal Records.. 501-371-4654
    Desk Officer.. 501-371-4605
    Detective Divisions
        Downtown. 501-371-4660
            Auto Theft.. 501-371-4449
            Homicide. 501-371-6870
                Cold Case Homicide. 501-371-4473
            Larceny.. 501-371-6883
            Robbery. 501-371-4674
        Northwest.. 501-918-3502
            Domestic Violence.. 501-918-3526
            Juvenile. 501-918-3538
            Victim Assistance.. 501-918-3504
        Southwest.. 501-918-3950
            Financial Crimes. 501-918-3970

Field Services. 501-371-4621
Impound Lot. 501-918-4260
Internal Affairs. 501-918-4285
Neighborhood Watch Coordinator. 501-918-5369
Patrol Divisions
      Downtown. 501-918-5130
      Northwest 501-918-3500
      Southwest 501-918-3900
Public Affairs 501-371-4626
Records. 501-371-4654
School Resource Officers 501-379-1521
Special Investigations/Narcotics-Vice. 501-918-3800
Special Operations. 501-918-5100
Training. 501-918-4300
Warrants. 501-371-4642
Locksburn (Sevier Co. Sheriff). 870-642-2125
London. 479-293-4115
Lonoke. 501-676-6953
Lonsdale (Garland Co. Sheriff). 501-622-3660
Louann (Ouachita Co. Sheriff). 870-837-2200
Lowell (City Hall). 479-659-8976
Luxora (City Hall). 870-658-2629
Lynn (Lawrence Co. Sheriff). 870-886-2525

Madison (St. Francis Co. Sheriff). 870-633-2611
Magazine. 479-969-0809
Magness (Independence Co. Sheriff). 870-793-8838
Magnet Cove (Hot Spring Co. Sheriff). 501-332-3671
Magnolia. 870-234-5655
Malvern. 501-332-3636
Mammoth Spring. 870-625-7516
Manila. 870-561-4777
Mansfield (City Hall). 479-928-5700
Marble Falls (Newton Co. Sheriff). 870-446-5124
Marianna. 870-295-2508
Marie (Mississippi Co. Sheriff). 870-658-2242
Marion. 870-739-2101
Marked Tree. 870-358-2024
Marmaduke (City Hall). 870-597-2020
Marshall (Searcy Co. Sheriff). 870-448-2340
Marvell. 870-829-3271
Maumelle. 501-851-1337
Mayflower. 501-470-1000
Maynard (Randolph Co. Sheriff). 870-892-8888

McCaskill (Hempstead Co. Sheriff)............................ 870-777-6727
McCrory... 870-731-2421
McDougal (Clay Co. Sheriff)................................... 870-598-2270
McGehee... 870-222-3636
McNab (Hempstead Co. Sheriff)................................. 870-777-6727
McNeil (Columbia Co. Sheriff)................................. 870-234-5331
McRae (Beebe P.D.).. 501-882-3365
Melbourne (Izard Co. Sheriff)................................. 870-368-4203
Mena.. 479-394-1212
Menifee... 501-354-6598
Midland (Sebastian Co. Sheriff).............................. 479-783-1051
Mineral Springs.. 870-287-4500
Minturn (Lawrence Co. Sheriff)............................... 870-886-2525
Mitchellville (Desha Co. Sheriff)............................ 870-877-2327
Monette (Craighead Co. Sheriff).............................. 870-933-4550
Monticello... 870-367-3411
Montrose (Ashley Co. Sheriff)................................ 870-853-2040
Moorefield (Independence Co. Sheriff)........................ 870-793-8838
Moro (Lee Co. Sheriff)....................................... 870-295-7777
Morrilton.. 501-354-0131
Morrison Bluff (Logan Co. Sheriff)........................... 479-963-3271
Mount Holly (Union Co. Sheriff).............................. 870-864-1970
Mount Ida (Montgomery Co. Sheriff)........................... 870-867-3151
Mount Pleasant (Izard Co. Sheriff)........................... 870-368-4203
Mount Vernon... 501-849-2828
Mountain Home.. 870-425-6336
Mountain Pine (Garland Co. Sheriff).......................... 501-622-3660
Mountain View.. 870-269-4211
Mountainburg (Crawford Co. Sheriff).......................... 479-474-2261
Mulberry (Alma Police)....................................... 479-632-3333
Murfreesboro... 870-285-3533

Nashville.. 870-845-3434
Natural Dam (Crawford Co. Sheriff)........................... 479-474-2261
New Edinburg (Cleveland Co. Sheriff)......................... 870-325-6222
Newark (Independence Co. Sheriff)............................ 870-793-8838
Newport.. 870-523-2721
Nimmons (Clay Co. Sheriff)................................... 870-598-2270
Norfork (Baxter Co. Sheriff)................................. 870-425-2400
Norman (Montgomery Co. Sheriff).............................. 870-867-3151
Norphlet (Union Co. Sheriff)................................. 870-864-1970
North Little Rock (www.nlrpolice.org/)....................... 501-758-1234
        Chief of Police...................................... 501-771-7101
        Desk... 501-771-7117

Detectives

    Crimes Against Persons. 501-771-7150

    Property Crimes. 501-771-7160

    Juvenile, Financial, Sex, and Battery. 501-771-7162

    Narcotics. 501-758-5432

    Cold Cases 501-351-1442

Criminal Records. 501-771-7119

Substations

    Patrol Commander. 501-771-7171

    Broadway. 501-376-3407

    Lakewood. 501-812-2690

    Levy. 501-791-2060

    Main Street. 501-376-3407

    Rose City. 501-945-8136

Professional Standards. 501-771-7107

Public Information Officer. 501-771-7109

Warrants. 501-771-7127

Oak Grove (Carroll Co. Sheriff). 870-423-2901

Oak Grove Heights (Greene Co. Sheriff). 870-236-7612

Oakhaven (Hempstead Co. Sheriff). 870-777-6727

Oden (Montgomery Co. Sheriff). 870-867-3151

Ogden (Little River Co. Sheriff). 870-898-5115

Oil Trough (Independence Co. Sheriff). 870-793-8838

O'Kean (Randolph Co. Sheriff). 870-892-8888

Okolona (Clark Co. Sheriff). 870-246-2222

Ola. 479-489-5612

Omaha.. 870-365-6356

Oppelo (City Hall). 501-354-2454

Osceola.. 870-563-5213

Oxford (Izard Co. Sheriff). 870-368-4203

Ozan (Hempstead Co. Sheriff). 870-777-6727

Ozark. 479-667-2233

Ozark Acres (Sharp Co. Sheriff). 870-994-2211

Palestine (St. Francis Co. Sheriff). 870-633-2611

Pangburn (City Hall).. 501-728-4611

Paragould (Greene Co. Sheriff). 870-236-7612

Paris. 479-963-2600

Parkdale (Ashley Co. Sheriff). 870-853-2040

Parkin (City Hall). 870-755-5491

Patmos (Hempstead Co. Sheriff). 870-777-6727

Patterson (City Hall).. 870-731-5057

Peach Orchard (Clay Co. Sheriff).. 870-598-2270

Pea Ridge. 479-451-8220
Perla (Hot Spring Co. Sheriff). 501-332-3671
Perry (City Hall).. 501-662-4571
Perrytown (Hempstead Co. Sheriff). 870-777-6727
Perryville (City Hall). 501-889-2862
Piggott.. 870-598-2295
Pindall (Searcy Co. Sheriff). 870-448-2340
Pine Bluff (www.pbpd.org/). 870-543-5100
Pineville (Izard Co. Sheriff). 870-368-4203
Plainview. 479-272-4000
Pleasant Plains (Independence Co. Sheriff). 870-793-8838
Plumerville. 501-354-6400
Pocahontas. 870-892-9867
Pollard (Clay Co. Sheriff). 870-598-2270
Portia (Lawrence Co. Sheriff). 870-886-2525
Portland (Ashley Co. Sheriff).. 870-853-2040
Pottsville. 479-968-2864
Powhatan (Lawrence Co. Sheriff). 870-886-2525
Poyen (Grant Co. Sheriff).. 870-942-2101
Prairie Grove. 479-846-3270
Prattsville (Grant Co. Sheriff). 870-942-2101
Prescott.. 870-887-6779
Pyatt (Marion Co. Sheriff). 870-449-4236

Quitman. 501-589-3512

Ratcliff (Logan Co. Sheriff). 479-963-3271
Ravenden (Lawrence Co. Sheriff). 870-886-2525
Ravenden Springs (Randolph Co. Sheriff). 870-892-8888
Reader (Ouachita Co. Sheriff). 870-837-2200
Rector.. 870-595-2423
Redfield. 501-397-5100
Reed (Desha Co. Sheriff). 870-877-2327
Reyno (Randolph Co. Sheriff). 870-892-8888
Rison (City Hall). 870-325-6381
Rockport. 501-332-8700
Roe (Monroe Co. Sheriff).. 870-747-3811
Rogers. 479-636-4141
Romance (White Co. Sheriff). 501-268-3543
Rondo (Lee Co. Sheriff). 870-295-7777
Rose Bud (City Hall). 501-556-4967
Rosston (Nevada Co. Sheriff).. 870-887-2616
Rudy (Crawford Co. Sheriff). 479-474-2261
Russell (White Co. Sheriff). 501-268-3543

Russellville. 479-968-3232

Salem. 870-895-3874
Salesville (City Hall). 870-499-5675
Scotland (Van Buren Co. Sheriff). 501-745-2112
Scranton (Logan Co. Sheriff). 479-963-3271
Searcy. 501-268-3531
Sedgewick (Lawrence Co. Sheriff). 870-886-2525
Shannon Hills. 501-455-3125
Sheridan. 870-942-5512
Sherrill (Jefferson Co. Sheriff). 870-541-5351
Sherwood (www.sherwoodpolice.org/). 501-835-1425
    Administration. 501-835-1425
    Criminal Investigation Division. 501-834-8799
    Division 2. 501-835-0954
    Division 3. 501-833-9322
    Division 4. 501-835-0113
    Division 5. 501-835-3568
    Patrol. 501-835-1425
    Warrants. 501-835-9074
Shirley (Van Buren Co. Sheriff). 501-745-2112
Sidney (Sharp Co. Sheriff) 870-994-2211
Siloam Springs. 479-524-4118
Smackover. 870-725-3571
Smithville (Lawrence Co. Sheriff). 870-886-2525
South Lead Hill (Diamond City P.D.). 870-422-7589
Sparkman (Dallas Co. Sheriff). 870-352-2002
Springdale. 479-751-4542
    Criminal Investigation Division. 479-750-8139
Springtown (Benton Co. Sheriff). 479-273-5532
St. Charles (City Hall). 870-282-3425
St. Francis (Clay Co. Sheriff). 870-598-2270
St. Joe (Searcy Co. Sheriff). 870-448-2340
St. Paul (Madison Co. Sheriff). 479-738-2320
Stamps. 870-533-4991
Star City (City Hall). 870-628-4244
Stephens. 870-786-5480
Strawberry (Lawrence Co. Sheriff). 870-886-2525
Strong (Union Co. Sheriff). 870-864-1970
Stuttgart. 870-673-1414
Subiaco (Logan Co. Sheriff). 479-963-3271
Success (Clay Co. Sheriff). 870-598-2270
Sulphur Rock (Independence Co. Sheriff). 870-793-8838
Sulphur Springs. 479-298-7773

Summitt (Marion Co. Sheriff)........................... 870-449-4236
Sunset (Crittenden Co. Sheriff)......................... 870-702-2000
Swifton.. 870-485-2600

Taylor... 870-234-5655
Texarkana AR (arkpolice.txkusa.org/) 903-798-3130
    Crimes Against Persons........................... 903-798-3156
    Crimes Against Property.......................... 903-798-3303
    Criminal Investigation Division.................. 903-798-3133
    Narcotics.. 903-798-3555
    Patrol... 903-798-3560
    Special Operations............................... 870-779-1711
    Warrants... 903-798-3086
Texarkana TX (http://www.texarkanapolice.com/). 903-798-3116
Thornton (Calhoun Co. Sheriff). 870-798-2323
Tillar (Drew Co. Sheriff).............................. 870-367-6211
Tinsman (Calhoun Co. Sheriff).......................... 870-798-2323
Tollette (Howard Co. Sheriff). 870-845-2626
Tontitown (Washington Co. Sheriff)..................... 479-444-5700
Traskwood (Saline Co. Sheriff)......................... 501-303-5642
Trumann... 870-483-6423
Tuckerman... 870-349-2424
Tull (Grant Co. Sheriff).............................. 870-942-2101
Tupelo (Jackson Co. Sheriff).......................... 870-523-5842
Turrell... 870-343-8621
Twin Groves (Faulkner Co. Sheriff).................... 501-328-5906
Tyronza (City Hall). 870-487-2168

Ulm (Prairie Co. Sheriff). 870-256-4137
Union Town (Crawford Co. Sheriff). 479-474-2261

Valley Springs (Boone Co. Sheriff). 870-741-8404
Van Buren... 479-474-1234
Vandervoort (Polk Co. Sheriff). 479-394-2511
Victoria (Mississippi Co. Sheriff). 870-658-2242
Vilonia... 501-796-8170
Viola (Fulton Co. Sheriff)............................ 870-895-2601

Wabbaseka... 870-766-8313
Waldenburg (Poinsett Co. Sheriff). 870-578-5411
Waldo... 870-693-5315
Waldron... 479-637-9106
Walnut Ridge.. 870-886-3568
Ward.. 501-843-6351

Warren. 870-226-3703
Washington (Hempstead Co. Sheriff). 870-777-6727
Watson (Desha Co. Sheriff). 870-877-2327
Weiner (City Hall). 870-684-2284
Weldon (Jackson Co. Sheriff).. 870-523-5842
West Fork. 479-839-2300
West Memphis (www.westmemphispolice.com/). 870-735-1210
     Chief of Police. 870-732-7652
     Criminal Investigation Division. 870-732-7525
     Narcotics. 770-732-7540
     Patrol. 870-732-7555
West Point (White Co. Sheriff).. 501-268-3543
Western Grove (Newton Co. Sheriff).. 870-446-5124
Wheatley (St. Francis Co. Sheriff). 870-633-2611
Whelen Springs (Clark Co. Sheriff). 870-246-2222
White Hall. 870-247-1414
Wicks (Polk Co. Sheriff). 479-394-2511
Widener (St. Francis Co. Sheriff).. 870-633-2611
Wiederkehr Village (Franklin Co. Sheriff).. 479-667-4127
Williford (Sharp Co. Sheriff).. 870-994-2211
Willisville (Nevada Co. Sheriff). 870-887-2616
Wilmar (Drew Co. Sheriff). 870-367-6211
Wilmot (Ashley Co. Sheriff).. 870-853-2040
Wilson (Mississippi Co. Sheriff). 870-658-2242
Wilton (Little River Co. Sheriff). 870-898-5115
Winchester (Drew Co. Sheriff).. 870-367-6211
Winslow (Washington Co. Sheriff).. 479-444-5700

Winthrop (Little River Co. Sheriff). 870-898-5115
Wooster (Faulkner Co. Sheriff). 501-328-5906
Wynne.. 870-238-8718

Yellville (Marion Co. Sheriff). 870-449-4236

Zinc (Boone Co. Sheriff). 870-741-8404

ARKANSAS ASSOCIATION OF CHIEFS OF POLICE

P.O. Box 251825   501-372-4600
Little Rock 72225. . . . . fax 501-372-4505

CORONERS

Arkansas	870-946-3104
Ashley	870-853-5252
Baxter	870-425-3288
Benton	479-621-0223
Boone	870-741-0016
Bradley	870-226-2633
Calhoun	870-310-4654
Carroll	870-423-4253
Chicot	870-265-6166
Clark	870-230-1400
Clay	870-598-3469
Cleburne	870-834-1107
Cleveland	870-325-6216
Columbia	870-234-2802
Conway	501-354-1638
Craig head	870-932-9639
Crawford	479-806-5959
Crittenden	870-735-5855
Cross	870-238-7237
Dallas	870-352-3131
Desha	870-377-1250
Drew	870-367-2451
Faulkner	501-450-4917
Franklin	479-667-4712
Fulton	870-895 3990
Garland	501-622-3638
Grant	870-942-1306
Green	870-450-5132
Hempstead	870-777-6772
Hot Springs	501-467-3030
Howard	870-451-0400
Independence	870-793-8848
Izard	870-368-4848
Jackson	870-523-5822
Jefferson	870-541-5364
Johnson	479-754-8178
Lafayette	870-921-5896
Lawrence	870-759-0382
Lee	870-295-9619
Lincoln	870-628-4204
Little River	870-898-3331
Logan	479-963-3271

Lonoke.	501-843-3051
Madison.	479-738-2621
Marion.	870-449-6621
Miller.	870-774-1200
Mississippi.	870-563-6578
Monroe.	870-734-1211
Montgomery.	870-867-2001
Nevada.	870-703-0138
Newton.	870-420-3552
Ouachita.	870-836-2168
Perry.	501-889-3310
Phillips.	870-572-3336
Pike.	870-285-2305
Poinsett.	870-578-5441
Polk.	479-394-4477
Pope.	479-968-2558
Prairie.	870-255-3760
Pulaski.	501-340-8355
Randolph.	870-892-5242
Saline.	501-303-1559
Scott.	479-637-3001
Searcy.	870-448-5118
Sebastian.	479-783-0630
Sevier.	870-584-8101
Sharp.	870-847-0128
St. Francis.	870-633-5400
Stone.	870-269 3210
Union.	870-864-1903
Van Buren.	501-745-8217
Washington	479-521-5000
White.	501-268-7220
Woodruff.	870-347-2576
Yell.	479-495-2525

COLLEGE AND UNIVERSITY
POLICE AND SECURITY

Arkansas Baptist College, Little Rock. 501-374-7856
Arkansas Northeastern College
       Blythville (main). 870-762-3158
       Osceola Center. 870-563-3236
       Pargould Center. 870-239-3200
Arkansas State University
       Beebe. 501-882-8251
       Jonesboro (main). 870-972-2093
       Mountain Home. 870-508-6122
       Newport. 870-512-7866
       Tech Center. 870-358-2117
Arkansas Tech University
       Russellville (main). 479-968-0222
       Ozark. 866-225-2884
Black River Technical College
       Pocahontas (main). . . . . 870-248-4000 ext 4034
       Paragould 870-239-0969
Central Baptist College, Conway. 501-329-6872
Clinton School of Public Service (U of A). 501-683-5200
Cossatot Community College, DeQueen. . . . . 870-584-4471 ext 137
Crowley's Ridge College, Paragould 870-236-6901
East Arkansas Community College, Forrest City. 870-633-4480
Ecclesia College, Springdale. 479-248-7236
Embry-Riddle Aeronautical University, LRAFB. 501-983-9300
Freedom Bible College & Seminary, Rogers 800-494-7497
Harding University, Searcy. 501-279-5000
Henderson State University, Arkadelphia. 870-230-5098
Hendrix College, Conway. 501-450-1467
John Brown University, Siloam Springs. 479-524-7403
Lyon College, Batesville. 870-698-4265
Mid-South Community College, West Memphis. 870-733-6722
National Park Community College, Hot Springs. 501-760-4293
North Arkansas College. 870-391-3124
North Arkansas Community College, Harrison. 479-619-4229
NorthWest Arkansas Community College, Bentonville. 479-636-9222
Ouachita Technical College, Malvern . . . . 501-337-5000 ext 1120
Ozarka College, Melbourne. 870-368-2032
Philander Smith College, Little Rock. 501-370-5354
Phillips Community College, Helena-West Helena . . . . 870-338-6474 ext 1235
Pulaski Technical College
       North Little Rock (main). . . . . 501-812-2711, cell 501-580-1831

Little Rock South. . . . . cell 501-626-7152
Little Rock West. . . . . cell 501-580-1662
Business and Industry Center, Little Rock. 501-907-6670
Aerospace Technology Center, North Little Rock. 501-835-5420
Saline County Career Center . . . . 501-602-2420, cell 501-580-0521
Remington College, Little Rock. 501-232-4294
Rich Mountain Community College, Mena. 479-394-7622
Shorter College, North Little Rock. 501-374-6305
South Arkansas Community College, El Dorado. 870-864-7125
Southeast Arkansas College, Pine Bluff. 870-543-5900
Southern Arkansas University, Magnolia. 870-235-4100
Southern Arkansas University Tech, Camden. 870-574-4517
University of Arkansas, Clinton School of Public Service. 501-683-5200
University of Arkansas, Fayetteville. 479-575-2222
University of Arkansas at Fort Smith. 479-788-7141
University of Arkansas at Little Rock. 501-569-3400
University of Arkansas Medical Sciences
　　　Little Rock (main). 501-686-7777
　　　AHEC Fayetteville. 479-521-8269
University of Arkansas at Monticello. 870-460-1083
University of Arkansas at Pine Bluff. 870-575-8102
University of Arkansas Community College
　　　Batesville. 870-612-2039
　　　Hope. 870-777-5722
　　　Morrilton. 501-977-2065
University of Central Arkansas. 501-450-3111
University of the Ozarks, Clarksville. 479-979-2020
Webster University, Little Rock. 501-375-1511
Williams Baptist College, Walnut Ridge. . . . . 870-759-4161 & 870-679-9239

ARKANSAS HOSPITALS
(including Texarkana TX and Memphis TN)
These are main numbers; few publicize their security or police numbers

Advance Care Hospital–Ft. Smith
    7301 Rogers Ave., 4th Fl., Ft. Smith 72903. 479-314-4900
Advance Care Hospital–Hot Springs
    300 Werner St., Third Fl., Hot Springs 71913. 501-609-4300
Ashley County Medical Center
    1015 Unity Road, Crossett 71635. 870-364-4111
Arkansas Children's Hospital
    800 Marshall St. Little Rock 72202. 501-364-1100
Arkansas Heart Hospital
    1701 S. Shackleford Rd,, Little Rock 72211. 501-219-7000
Arkansas Methodist Medical Center
    900 W. Kings Hwy., Paragould 72450. 870-239-7100
Arkansas State Hospital
    4313 W. Markham St., Little Rock 72205. 501-686-9000

Baptist Health Medical Center
    9601 Interstate 630, Little Rock 72205.. 501-202-2000
Baptist Health Medical Center–Arkadelphia
    3050 Twin Rivers Dr., Arkadelphia 71923. 870-245-2622
Baptist Health Medical Center–Heber Springs
    2319 Hwy. 110 W., Heber Springs 72543. 501-887-3000
Baptist Health Medical Center–North Little Rock
    3333 Springhill Dr., N. Little Rock 72114. 501-202-3000
Baptist Health Rehabilitation Institute
    9601 Interstate 630, Little Rock 72205.. 501-663-3302
Baxter Regional Medical Center
    624 Hospital Drive, Mountain Home 72653.. 870-508-1000
Booneville Community Hospital
    880 W. Main St., Bonneville 72927. 479-675-2800
Bradley County Medical Center
    404 S. Bradley St., Warren 71671. 870-226-4302
BridgeWay
    21 Bridgeway Rd., North Little Rock 72113. 501-771-1500

Chicot Memorial Hospital
    2729 Hwy. 65 & 82, Lake Village 71653.. 870-265-5351
Christus St. Michael Health System
    2600 St. Michael Dr., Texarkana, TX 75503. 903-614-1000
Community Medical Center of Izard County
    103 Grasse St., Calico Rock 72519. 870-297-3726

Conway Regional Medical Center
2302 College Ave., Conway 72032. 501-450-2117
Crittenden Memorial Hospital
200 W. Tyler Ave., West Memphis 72301. 870-735-1500
CrossRidge Community Hospital
310 S. Falls Blvd., Wynne 72396. 870-238-3300

Dallas County Medical Center
201 N. Clifton, Fordyce 71742. 870-352-6300
Delta Memorial Hospital
811 Hwy. 65 S., Dumas 71639. 870-382-8126
De Queen Regional Medical Center
1306 W. Collin Raye, De Queen 71832. 870-584-0272
DeWitt Hospital
1641 S. Whitehead Drive, DeWitt 72042. 870-233-2208
Drew Memorial Hospital
778 Scogin Drive, Monticello 71655. 870-367-2411
Dubuis Hospital Of Texarkana
2400 St Michael Dr #2, Texarkana TX 75503. 903-614-1000

Eureka Springs Hospital
24 Norris, Eureka Springs 72632. 479-253-7400

Fulton County Hospital
679 N. Main St., Salem 72576. 870-895-6099

Great River Medical Center
1520 N. Division, Blytheville 72315. 870-838-7460

Harris Hospital
1205 McLain, Newport 72112. 870-512-3022
HealthPark Hospital
1636 Higdon Ferry Rd., Hot Springs 71913. 501-520-2000
Healthsouth Rehabilitation of Fayetteville
153 Monte Painter Dr., Fayetteville 72702. 479-444-2200
HealthSouth Rehabilitation Hospital of Jonesboro
1201 Fleming Ave., Jonesboro 72401. 870-932-0440
HealthSouth Rehabilitation Hospital of Texarkana
515 West 12th St., Texarkana, TX 75501. 903-793-0088
Helena Regional Medical Center
101 Newman Dr., Helena-W.Helena 72342. 870-338-5800
Hot Spring County Medical Center
1001 Schneider Drive, Malvern 72104. 501-332-1003

Howard Memorial Hospital
 800 W. Leslie Nashville 71852. 870-845-8003

Jefferson Regional Medical Center
 600 W. 40th Ave., Pine Bluff 71603.. 870-541-7100
John Ed Chambers Memorial Hospital Inc.
 Highway 10 at Detroit, Danville 72833. 479-495-2241
Johnson Regional Medical Center
 1100 E. Poplar St., Clarksville 72830.. 479-754-5454

Lawrence Memorial Hospital
 1309 W. Main St., Walnut Ridge 72476.. 870-886-1200
Levi Hospital
 300 Prospect Ave., Hot Springs 71901. 501-760-3322
Little River Memorial Hospital
 451 W. Locke St., Ashdown 71822. 870-898-5011
Living Hope Hospital of Texarkana
 801 Arkansas Blvd., Texarkana 71854.. 870-774-4673

Magnolia City Hospital
 101 Hospital Drive, Magnolia 71753.. 870-235-3000
Mena Regional Health System
 311 N. Morrow, Mena 71953.. 479-243-2369
Medical Center of South Arkansas
 700 W. Grove, El Dorado 71730. 870-863-2000
Medical Park Hospital
 2001 S. Main, Hope 71801.. 870-777-2323
Mercy Hospital of Scott County
 895 W. Sixth St., Waldron 72958.. 479-637-4135
Mercy Hospital/Turner Memorial
 801 W. River St., Ozark 72949. 479-667-4138

National Park Medical Center
 1910 Malvern Ave., Hot Springs 71901.. 501-321-1000
NEA Medical Center
 3024 Stadium Blvd., Jonesboro 72401.. 870-972-7000
NMC-Willow Creek Women's Hospital
 4301 Greathouse Sprgs Rd, Johnson 72741.. 479-684-3000
North Arkansas Regional Medical Center
 620 N. Willow, Harrison 72601.. 870-365-2000
North Logan Mercy Hospital
 500 E. Academy St., Paris 72855.. 479-963-6101
Northwest Medical Center–Springdale
 609 W. Maple, Springdale 72764.. 479-757-4005

Northwest Medical Center–Bentonville
    3000 Medical Ctr. Pkwy, Bentonville 72712.................... 479-553-1000

Ouachita County Medical Center
    638 California Ave. S.W., Camden 71701...................... 870-836-1000
Ozark Health Medical Center
    2500 Hwy. 65 S., Clinton 72031. 501-745-7000

Piggott Community Hospital
    1206 Gordon Duckworth Dr., Piggott 72454. 870-598-3881
Pike County Memorial Hospital
    315 E. 13th St., Murfreesboro 71958........................ 870-285-3182

Randolph County Medical Center
    2801 Medical Ctr. Dr., Pocahontas 72455.................... 870-892-6000
Rebsamen Medical Center
    1400 Braden St., Jacksonville 72076........................ 501-985-7000

River Valley Medical Center
    200 N. Third St., Dardanelle 72832......................... 479-229-4677

St. Anthony's Medical Center
    4 Hospital Drive, Morrilton 72110. 501-977-2300
St. Bernards Medical Center
    225 E. Jackson Ave., Jonesboro 72401. 870-972-4100
St. Edward Mercy Medical Center
    7301 Rogers Ave., Fort Smith 72917........................ 479-314-6000
St. John's Hospital–Berryville
    214 Carter St., Berryville 72616. 870-423-3355
St. Mary's Hospital
    1200 W. Walnut, Rogers 72756............................. 479-636-0200
St. Mary's Regional Medical Center
    1808 W. Main St., Russellville 72801....................... 479-968-2841
St. Joseph's Mercy Health Center
    300 Werner St., Hot Springs 71903. 501-622-1000
St. Vincent Infirmary Medical Center
    2 St. Vincent Circle, Little Rock 72205. 501-552-3000
St. Vincent Infirmary Medical Center–North
    2215 Wildwood Ave., Sherwood 72116. 501-552-7102
St. Vincent Rehabilitation Hospital
    2201 Wildwood Ave., Sherwood 72120. 501-834-1800
Saline Memorial Hospital
    1 Medical Park Drive, Benton 72015........................ 501-776-6000

Siloam Springs Memorial Hospital
205 E. Jefferson, Siloam Springs 72761................ 479-524-4141
SMC Regional Medical Center
1520 N Division St. Blytheville 72315. 870-838-7460
Southwest Regional Medical Center
11401 Interstate 30, Little Rock 72209................. 501-455-7100
Sparks Health System
1001 Towson Ave., Fort Smith 72901.................. 479-441-4000
Stone County Medical Center
2106 E. Main St., Mountain View 72560................ 870-269-4361
Summit Medical Center
East Main & S. 20th, Van Buren 72956. 479-474-3401
Stuttgart Regional Medical Center
1703 N. Buerkle Road, Stuttgart 72160................ 870-673-3511
Surgical Hospital of Jonesboro
909 Enterprise Drive, Jonesboro 72401................ 870-336-1100

United Methodist Behavioral Hospital
1601 Murphy Drive, Maumelle 72113.................. 501-803-3388
University of Arkansas for Medical Sciences
4301 W. Markham, Little Rock 72205................. 501-851-4623

Veterans Hospital–LR
John L. McClellan Memorial
4300 West Seventh, Little Rock 72205................. 501-257-1000
Veterans Hospital NLR
Eugene J. Towbin Healthcare Center
2200 Ft. Roots Dr., North Little Rock 72114........... 501-257-1000
Veterans Hospital–Fayetteville
Veterans Health Care System of the Ozarks
1100 N College Avenue, Fayetteville 72703............ 479-443-4301
Vista Health–Fayetteville
4253 N. Crossover Rd., Fayetteville 72703............. 479-494-5760
Vista Health–Fort Smith
10301 Mayo Road, Fort Smith 72923.................. 866-813-4673

Wadley Regional Medical Center
1000 Pine Street, Texarkana, TX 75501................ 903-798-8000
Washington Regional Medical Center
321 N. Hills Blvd., Fayetteville 72703. 479-713-1000
White County Medical Center
3214 E. Race Ave., Searcy 72143. 501-268-9863
White River Medical Center
1710 Harrison, Batesville 72501..................... 870-698-6545

MEMPHIS TENNESSEE HOSPITALS

Baptist Memorial Hospital–Memphis
     6019 Walnut Grove Rd., Memphis 38120. 901-226-5000
Delta Medical Center
     3000 Getwell Rd., Memphis 38118. 901-369-6010
Le Bonheur Children's Hospital
     50 N. Dunlap Street, Memphis 38103. 901-287-7337
Methodist Extended Care Hospital
     225 South Claybrook, Memphis 38104. 901-516-2595
Methodist Fayette Hospital
     214 Lakeview Drive, Somerville 38068. 901-516-4000
Methodist North Hospital
     3960 New Covington Pike, Memphis 38128. 901-516-5766
Methodist South Hospital
     1300 Wesley Drive, Memphis 38116. 901-516-3700
Methodist University Hospital
     1265 Union Ave., Memphis 38104. 901-516-7000
Regional Medical Center at Memphis (The "Med")
     877 Jefferson Ave, Memphis 38103. 901-545-7100
St. Jude Children's Research Hospital
     262 Danny Thomas Place, Memphis 38105 901-576-6683
University of Tennessee Health Science Center
     920 Madison Ave., Memphis 38163. 901-448-5500
Veteran's Administration Medical Center
     1030 Jefferson Ave., Memphis 38104. 901-523-8990

FEDERAL LAW ENFORCEMENT

FEDERAL BUREAU OF INVESTIGATION
www.fbi.gov

FBI Little Rock, Arkansas Field Office
24 Shackleford West Boulevard. 501-221-9100

El Dorado Resident Agency
Regions Bank, Suite 205
100 East Peach Street
El Dorado, AR 71730
870-863-3466
fax 870-863-5172

Fayetteville Resident Agency
75 N. East Avenue, Suite 201
Fayetteville, AR 72701
479-443-3181
fax 479-443-3274

Fort Smith Resident Agency
1501 S. Waldron Rd, # 209
Fort Smith, AR 72903
479-452-5873
fax 479-478-7170

Hot Springs Resident Agency
324 Malvern Ave, Room 200
Hot Springs, AR 71901
501-321-2544
fax 501-321-0986

Jonesboro Resident Agency
Regions Bank, Third Floor
2400 E. Highland Drive
Jonesboro, AR 72401
870-932-0700
fax 870-932-0918

Marion Resident Agency
2840 Interstate 55
Marion, AR 72364
870-739-4651
fax 870-739-4673

Pine Bluff Resident Agency
3115 Federal Building
100 East 8th Street
Pine Bluff, AR 71601
870-535-4580
fax 870-535-4841

Texarkana Resident Agency
214 Federal Building
500 North State Line Ave.
Texarkana, AR 71854
870-774-7682
870-772-8196

U.S. MARSHALS

Note: (1) also listed under Federal Courts and Jails. (2) Full U.S. directory at
http://www.leadershipdirectories.com/images/sp/sp_fryb.pdf (dated, but still helpful)

Eastern District of Arkansas:

A328 U.S. Courthouse
     600 West Capitol, Little Rock 72201 501-324-6256
                                            fax 501-324-6252
615 South Main, Jonesboro 72401. 870-972-4611
                                            fax 870-972-4690
Not staffed unless court in session:
     490 College Street, Batesville 72501 501-324-6256
     617 Walnut Street, Helena-West Helena 72342. 501-324-6256
     100 E. Eighth Street, Pine Bluff 71601. 501-324-6256

Western District of Arkansas:

243 Federal Building
30 S. Sixth Street, Fort Smith 72901.. 479-783-5215
                                            fax 479-782-4690
202 U.S. P.O. & Courthouse
101 S. Jackson, El Dorado 71730. 870-863-4734
                                            fax 870-863-7726
516 Federal Building
35 E. Mountain St., Fayetteville 72701. 479-442-6141
                                            fax 479-443-1674
352 Federal Building
100 Reserve St., Hot Springs 71901.. 501-623-9547
                                            fax 501-321-9613
Federal Building
500 Stateline Ave. Texarkana 75501. 870-774-9922

U.S. MARSHAL'S ARKANSAS
PRETRIAL DETENTION FACILITIES
(See the county jail listings for address and phone number)

Eastern District (DUSM Lynn Oller):

Dallas County Jail
Faulkner County Jail
Jefferson County Jail
Lonoke County Jail
Pulaski County Regional Detention Facility
Sheridan Detention Center
Van Buren County Jail
White County Jail

occasionally:
> West Tennessee Detention Facility (mostly awaiting airlift)
> > Corrections Corp. of America
> > 6299 Finde Naifeh Dr., P.O. Box 509. 901-294-3060
> > Mason, TN 38049. . . . . fax 901-294-2936
> Craighead County Jail

Western District:

Benton County
Bowie County Correctional Center
> 105 West Front Street
> Texarkana, TX 75501. 903-798-3505
Garland County (overnight)
Miller County
Scott County
Sebastian County
Texarkana City Jail
> 100 North Stateline Ave.
> Texarkana, TX 75501. 903-798-3199
Union County
Washington County

BUREAU OF ALCOHOL, TOBACCO,
FIREARMS, AND EXPLOSIVES
http://www.atf.gov/

Little Rock Field Office
425 West Capitol, Room 775   501-324-6181
Little Rock 72201 . . . . fax 501-324-5301

Industry Operations.. 501-324-6457
                                                          fax 501-324-6695
Fort Smith Field Office
30 South 6th Street, Room B129A   501-709-0872
Fort Smith 72901 . . . . fax 501-709-0532

New Orleans Field Division
One Galleria Boulevard, Suite 1700   504-841-7000
Metairie, Louisiana 70001 .. . . fax 504-841-7039

DRUG ENFORCEMENT ADMINISTRATION
http://www.justice.gov/dea/index.htm

Fayetteville.. 479-442-2618
        179 East Colt Drive Fayetteville 72703

Fort Smith. 479-783-6300
        30 South 6th St., B129a, Fort Smith 72901

Little Rock. 501-217-6500
        10825 Financial Centre Parkway, Little Rock 72211

Regional Office. 504-840-1100
        3838 N. Causeway Blvd., Suite 1800, Metairie, LA 70002

IMMIGRATION AND CUSTOMS ENFORCEMENT
http://www.ice.gov/

Immigration
4501 E. Roosevelt Road   501-370-2700
Little Rock 72206... fax 501-370-2764

Customs
10800 Financial Parkway, Suite 470
Little Rock 72211... 501-312-7000

Detainee Locator. .... http://locator.ice.gov/odls/homePage.do

SECRET SERVICE
www.secretservice.gov/

111 Center Street, Suite 1700, Little Rock 72201. 501-324-6241

INTERNAL REVENUE SERVICE
www.irs.gov

Criminal Investigation Division   501-396-5917
700 W. Capitol Ave., Little Rock 72201. .... fax 501-372-8304

POSTAL INSPECTION SERVICE
https://postalinspectors.uspis.gov/

Arkansas Office
2200 Fort Roots Drive
North Little Rock 72114
501-945-6720

Regional Office
650 N. Sam Houston Pkwy W
Houston, TX 77067-9000
877-876-2455

FEDERAL PROTECTIVE SERVICES

2200 Fort Roots Drive
North Little Rock 72114....................................... 501-324-5223

LITTLE ROCK AIR FORCE BASE
http://www.littlerock.af.mil/

Base Operator.. 501-987-1110
  Little Rock AFB 72099
OSI
Bldg. 1250. 501-987-6116
Security Forces
Bldg. 480, 314 SFS. 501-987-3221

PINE BLUFF ARSENAL
http://www.pba.army.mil/

Pine Bluff Arsenal
10020 Kabrich Circle
Pine Bluff 71602-9500 . . . . main number 870-540-3000
Security.. 870-540-3505

NATIONAL CENTER FOR TOXICOLOGICAL RESEARCH
http://www.fda.gov/AboutFDA/CentersOffices/NCTR/default.htm

National Center for Toxicological Research
U.S. Food and Drug Administration
3900 NCTR Road
Jefferson 72079. 870-543-7000

NCTR Security
  Bldg. NCTR-21, Room 100   870-543-7426
  Jefferson 72079. . . . . fax 870-543-7761

ARKANSAS NATIONAL GUARD
POLICE AND PUBLIC SAFETY
http://www.arguard.org/

Camp Robinson Fire & Police
  building 7200, North Little Rock 72199. 501-212-5280

Fort Chaffee Maneuver Training Center
  Building 2100, Greenwood 72936 479-484-2666

VETERANS ADMINISTRATION
HOSPITAL SYSTEM POLICE

Eugene J. Towbin Healthcare Center (Ft. Roots)
    2200 Fort Roots Dr., N. Little Rock 72114. 501-257-6550

John L. McClellan Memorial Veterans Hospital
    4300 West Seventh, Little Rock 72205.. 501-257-6550

Veterans Health Care System of the Ozarks
    1100 N College Avenue, Fayetteville 72703. . . . . 479-443-4301 ext 5163

SOCIAL SECURITY INSPECTOR GENERAL

Resident Agent   501-324-6554
700 West Capitol Ave., Little Rock. . . . . fax 501-324-6555

STATE DEPARTMENT

Resident office, North Little Rock. 501-833-0273

HOUSING AND URBAN DEVELOPMENT
OFFICE OF INSPECTOR GENERAL

700 West Capitol Ave., Little Rock 72201 501-324-5409

NATIONAL FOREST RANGERS
http://www.fs.fed.us/

Ozark-St. Francis National Forests
605 West Main
Russellville 72801
479-964-7200
http://www.fs.fed.us/oonf/
   ozark/index.html

Ouachita National Forest
P.O. Box 1270
Hot Springs 71902
501-321-5202
http://www.fs.fed.us/r8/ouachita/

NATIONAL PARK RANGERS

http://www.nps.gov/index.htm

Buffalo River National Park
Superintendent
Buffalo National River
402 N. Walnut, Suite 136
Harrison 72601
870-365-2700
http://www.nps.gov/buff/index.htm

Buffalo Point Ranger Station
870-449-4311

Pruitt Ranger Station
870-446-5373

Hot Springs National Park
101 Reserve St.
Hot Springs 71901
Visitor Center–501-620-6715
Superintendent's Office–501-623-2824
http://www.nps.gov/hosp/index.htm

Other Arkansas National Park Sites are:

Pea Ridge National Military Park
15930 E Highway 62
Garfield 72732
479-451-8122

Fort Smith National Historic Site
301 Parker Avenue
P.O. Box 1406 (72902)
Fort Smith 72901
479-783-3961

Arkansas Post National Memorial
1741 Old Post Road
Gillett 72055
870-548-2207
fax 870-548-2431

Little Rock Central High
2120 Daisy L. Bates Drive
Little Rock 72202
501-374-1957

Trail of Tears
National Trails Intermountain Region
P.O. Box 728
Santa Fe, NM 87504
505-988-6098
fax 505-986-5214

CLINTON PRESIDENTIAL LIBRARY AND MUSEUM

http://www.clintonlibrary.gov/

1200 President Clinton Avenue   501-374-4242
Little Rock 72201. . . . . fax 501-244-2883

MEXICAN CONSULATE
http://portal.sre.gob.mx/littlerock/

3500 South University Ave   501-372-6933
Little Rock 72204...................................... fax 501-372-6109

consulmexlir@comcast.net

NOTES

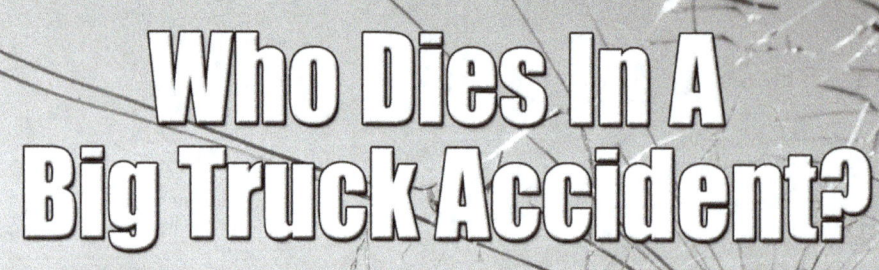

NOTES

Part III:

CORRECTIONS:
PRISONS, PROBATION,
AND JAILS
State, Local, and Federal

STATE

DEPARTMENT OF CORRECTION
http://www.adc.arkansas.gov/

Central Office

P.O. Box 8707
Pine Bluff 71611-8707
870-267-6999
fax 870-267-6258

Administrative Annex–East
2403 East Harding
Pine Bluff 71601
870-850-8510
fax 870-850-8550

Institutional Release Services
2801 S. Olive St. Suite 6-D
Pine Bluff 71603
870-543-1027
fax 870-879-6725

Pine Bluff Units

Pine Bluff Unit—ADC
890 Freeline Dr.
Pine Bluff 71603-1498
870-267-6510
fax 267-6523

Randall L. Williams Unit
7206 West 7th Street
Pine Bluff, AR 71603
870-267-6800
fax 870-879-2849

Former Diagnostic Unit—ADC
7500 Correction Circle
Pine Bluff 71603
870-267-6410
fax 870-267-6409

Wrightsville Units

Boot Camp
P.O. Box 1000
Wrightsville 72183-1000
501-897-2800
fax 501-897-1195

Hawkins Women's Unit
P.O. Box 1000
Wrightsville 72183-1000
501-897-2256
fax 501-897-2262

Wrightsville Unit
P.O. Box 1000
Wrightsville 72183-1000
501-897-5806
fax 501-897-5716

Grady Units

Cummins Unit
P.O. Box 500
Grady 71644-0500
870-850-8899
fax 870-850-8861

Varner Unit
P.O. Box 600
Grady 71644-0600
870-575-1800
fax 870-479-3803

Tucker Units

Tucker Unit
P.O. Box 240
Tucker 72168-0240
501-842-2519
fax 501-842-0351

Tucker Max
2501 State Farm Rd.
Tucker 72168-8713
501-842-3800
fax 501-842-1977

Newport Units

Grimes Unit (men)
300 Correction Drive
Newport 72112
870-523-5877
fax 870-523-8302

McPherson Unit (women)
302 Correction Drive
Newport 72112
870-523-2639
fax 870-523-6202

Other Units

East Arkansas Regional
P.O. Box 180
Brickeys 72320-0180
870-295-4700
fax 870-295-6564

Ouachita River Unit and Diagnostic
100 Walco Lane
Malvern 72104
501-467-3400
fax 501-467-3430

North Central Unit
10 Prison Circle
Calico Rock 72519-0300
870-297-4311
fax 870-297-4322

Delta Regional Unit
880 East Gaines
Dermott 71638-9505
870-538-2000
fax 870-538-2027

Texarkana Regional C.C.
305 East 5th Street
Texarkana 71854
870-779-3939
fax 870-779-1616

Benton Unit
6701 Highway 67
Benton 72015-8488
501-315-2252
fax 501-315-3736

Other Websites:
  Additional unit information:
    http://www.adc.arkansas.gov/facilities.html
  Inmate locator:
    http://www.adc.arkansas.gov/inmate_info/index.html

DEPARTMENT OF COMMUNITY CORRECTION
http://www.dcc.arkansas.gov/

Note: Further details or updates:
http://www.dcc.arkansas.gov/locations_area_offices_offices.html#RFCAC

Central Office:
105 W. Capitol Avenue, Suite 500
Little Rock 72201 501-682-9593

PAROLE BOARD
http://paroleboard.arkansas.gov/

Central Office:
105 W. Capitol Avenue, Suite 500
Little Rock 72201 501-682-3850
Pre-Release fax. 501-371-3550
Revocation fax. 501-682-3860
Administration/Fiscal fax. 501-683-5381
Press Inquires. 501-682-9593
Area Map:

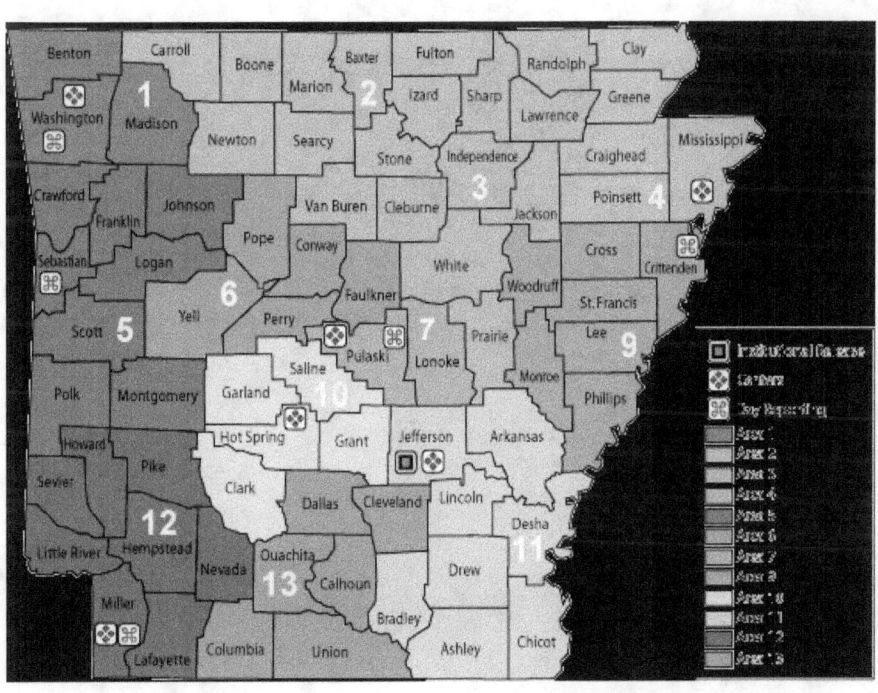

Area 1
Offices

Bentonville Area Office   479-464-0735
   703 S.E. "J" Street, Bentonville 72712 . . . . fax 479-464-0830

Benton County West/Parolee Intake and Supervision   479-696-0072
   1401 S.W. 14th Street, Bentonville 72712 . . . . fax 479-464-0830

Fayetteville Office   479-443-8000
   3416 N. College Ave, Suite 3, Fayetteville 72703 . . . . . . fax 479-443-7099

Residential Facilities

Northwest Arkansas Community Corrections Center   479-695-3400
114 N. College Ave, Fayetteville 72701 . . . . fax 479-443-1636

Institutional Release

Northwest Arkansas Work Release   479-756-2037
200 E. Price Ave, Springdale 72764 . . . . fax 479-756-0445

Area 2
Offices

Harrison Area Office   870-741-3228
   801 South Pine Street, Suite #1, Harrison 72601 . . . . fax 870-741-0028

Mountain Home Office   870-425-9139
   613 South Street, Mountain Home 72653 . . . . fax 870-424-5880

Salem Office   870-895-4411
   102 Pickren Street, P.O. Box 311, Salem 72576 . . . . fax 870-895-4540

Mountain View Office   870-269-5225
   301 Industrial Dr., Mountain View 72560 . . . . fax 870-269-4880

Berryville Office   870-423-5695
   504 Eureka Avenue, #C, Berryville 72616 . . . . fax 870-423-5330

Institutional Release

North Central Unit, ADC   870-297-4311
HC 62, Box 300, Calico Rock 72519 . . . . fax 870-297-4322

Area 3
Offices

Searcy Area Office   501-279-7990
     401 West Vine, Searcy 72143 . . . . fax 501-279-9156
     Parole, fax 501-279-3745

Newport Office   870-523-4191
     107 Laurel St. Newport 72112 . . . . fax 870-523-2557

Walnut Ridge Office   870-886-3553
     1000 W. Main St., Walnut Ridge 72476. . . . . fax 870-886-5488

Ash Flat Office   870-994-2977
     21A Court Drive, Mail: PO Box 224, Ash Flat 72513 . . . fax 870-994-7893

Heber Springs Office   501-362-3229
     1923 W. Main Heber Springs 72543 . . . . fax 501-362-3472

Batesville Office   870-793-7965
     913 25th St. Batesville 72501 . . . . fax 870-793-6796

Pocahontas Office   870-248-3330
     112 Pace Road, P.O. Box 554, Pocahontas 72455 . . . . . . fax 870-248-3332

Institutional Release
     Grimes Unit—ADC   870-523-5877
     300 Corrections Dr, Newport 72112 . . . . fax 870-217-0903

     McPherson Unit—ADC   870-523-2639
     302 Corrections Dr, Newport 72112 . . . . fax 870-217-0904

Area 4
Offices

Jonesboro Area Office   870-935-7290
     511 Union, Ste. 230, Courthouse Annex, Jonesboro 72401 fax 870-972-0910

Paragould Office   870-239-3192
     1011 Morgan Street, Paragould 72450 . . . . fax 870-236-9673

Osceola Office   870-563-5366
     1351 Cyro Road, Suite P, Osceola 72370 . . . . fax 870-563-6133

Residential Facilities
     Northeast Arkansas Community Corrections Center   870-563-8330
     1351 Cyro Road; PO Box 487, Osceola 72370 . . . . fax 870-563-4989

Institutional Release
     Mississippi County Work Release   870-762-1979
     727 North County Road 599, P.O. Box 10, Luxora 72358 . . . . fax 870-563-4989

Area 5
Offices
     Fort Smith Area Office   479-785-2664
     805 Garrison, Fort Smith 72901 . . . . fax 479-782-3146

     Booneville Office   479-675-3170
     42 East Main, Booneville 72927 . . . . fax 479-675-4084

     Clarksville Office   479-754-6200
     114 South Fulton, Clarksville 72830 . . . . fax 479-754-6497

     Ozark Office   479-667-9049
     118 S. 2nd Street, Ozark 72949 . . . . fax 479-394-4680

     Mena Office   479-394-4107
     500 DeQueen Street, Mena 71953 . . . . fax 479-394-4680

Area 6
Offices
     Conway Area Office   501-327-3256
     707 Robins Street, Suite 102, Conway 72032 . . . . fax 501-327-3299

     Russellville Office   501-968-5154
     1509 East Main Street, Suite 5, Russellville 72801 . . . . . fax 501-890-6854

     Morrilton Office   501-354-2164
     601 South Moose St., PO Box 800, Morrilton 72110 . . . . fax 501-354-2399

     Danville Office   479-495-5731
     110 W 6th St., Danville 72833 . . . . fax 479-495-5739

Area 7
Offices
     Little Rock Office   501-324-9176
     2679 Pike Ave, North Little Rock 72114 . . . . fax 501-371-1566
     2d floor fax 501-371-1567, 3d floor fax 501-371-0503

Lonoke Office   501-676-3378
    104 North East Front Street, Lonoke 72086 .... fax 501-676-3687

Residential Facilities
    Central Arkansas Community Corrections Center   501-686-9800
    4823 West 7th Street, Little Rock 72205 .... fax 501-686-9839

Area 9
Offices
    West Memphis Area Office   870-735-4486
        250 West Shoppingway, Suite B, West Memphis 72301   fax 870-735-4570

    Forrest City Office   870-630-1667
        409 N. Rosser Street, Suite B, Forrest City 72335 ...... fax 870-630-1746

    Helena Office   870-338-8931
        421 Perry Street, Helena 72342 .... fax 870-338-8946

Institutional Release
    East Arkansas Regional Unit—ADC   870-295-4700
    326 Lee 601, P.O. Box 180, Brickeys 72320 . ... fax 870-295-6564

Area 10
Offices
    Malvern Area Office   501-467-3633
        215 E. Highland, Malvern 72104 . ... fax 501-467-3378

    Benton Office   501-315-4477
        306 Edison, Suite 3, Benton 72015 .... fax 501-778-7825

    Arkadelphia Office   870-246-5960
        423 Crittenden St. Arkadelphia 71923 . ... fax 870-264-9106

    Sheridan Office   870-942-8451
        101 West Pine Street, Room # 3, Sheridan 72150 .... fax 870-942-1573

    Hot Springs Office   501-624-3347
        615 West Grand, Suite 2, Hot Springs 71901 .... fax 501-624-5057

Residential Facilities
    Omega Technical Violator Center   501-467-3041
    104 Walco Ln, Malvern 72104 .... fax 501-467-3053

Institutional Release

A.J. Hawkins Center–ADC	501-897-2800
22522 Asher Rd, P.O. Box 1010, Wrightsville 72183	fax 501-897-1195
Benton Unit—ADC	501-315-2252
6701 Highway 67, Benton 72015	fax 501-315-3736
Ouachita River Unit—ADC	501-467-3400
100 Walco Lane, P.O. Box 1630, Malvern 72104	fax 501-467-3431
Wrightsville Unit—ADC	501-897-5806
8400 Hwy 386, P.O. Box 407, Wrightsville 72183	fax 501-897-5716
Wrightsville Boot Camp—ADC	501-897-2256
22522 Asher Rd., P.O.Box 1010, Wrightsville 72183 . . .	fax 501-897-2262

Area 11

Offices

Pine Bluff Area Office	870-850-8950
2801 South Olive, Suite 6-D, Pine Bluff 71603	fax 870-536-4924
Stuttgart Office	870-673-8410
112 South Main, Stuttgart 72160	fax 870-673-2068
Star City Office	870-628-4882
200 West Wilcy Street, Star City 71667	fax not published
Monticello Office	870-367-3201
309 Hwy. 425 South, Monticello 71655	fax 870-367-2855
Crossett Office	870-304-2507
613 West First Ave., Crossett 71635	fax 870-304-2607

Residential Facilities

Southeast Arkansas Community Corrections Center	870-879-0661
7301 West 13th Street, Pine Bluff 71602	fax 870-879-2870

Institutional Release

Pine Bluff Unit—ADC	870-267-6510
890 Free Line Drive, Pine Bluff 71603	fax 870-267-6523
Diagnostic Unit—ADC	870-267-6410
7500 Correction Cir, Pine Bluff 72603	fax 870-267-6411

Randall L. Williams Correctional Facility—ADC 870-267-6800
7206 W. Seventh St, Pine Bluff 71603 . . . . fax 870-267-6563

Cummins Unit—ADC 870-850-8899
3001 Hwy 388, P.O.Box 500, Grady 71644 . . . . fax 870-850-8864

Varner Unit—ADC 870-575-1800
320 Hwy 388, P.O. Box 600, Grady 71644 . . . . fax 870-479-0043

Tucker Unit—ADC 501-842-2519
2401 State Farm Rd, Tucker 72168 . . . . fax 501-842-3958

Tucker Maximum Security Unit—ADC 501-842-3800
2501 State Farm Rd, Tucker 72168 . . . . fax 501-842-3958

Delta Regional Unit—ADC 870-538-2000
880 E. Gaines, Dermott 71638 . . . . fax 870-538-2027

Area 12
Offices
Texarkana Area Office 870-779-2000
    601 Hazel, Suite 6, Texarkana 71854 . . . . fax 870-779-2043

Ashdown Office 870-898-8870
    345 Keller Street, Ashdown 71822 . . . . fax 870-898-8872

De Queen Office. 870-642-4092
    511 W. Stillwell Ave., De Queen 71832 . . . . fax not published

Hope Office 870-777-2445
    2806 North Hazel, Hope 71801 . . . . fax 870-777-2170

Lewisville Office 870-921-5301
    110 East Fourth Street, Suite 10, Lewisville 71845 . . . . . fax 870-921-5333

Nashville Office 870-845-3793
    420 N. Main Street, Nashville 71852 . . . . fax 870-845-2572

Residential Facilities
Southwest Arkansas Community Corrections Center 870-779-2036
506 Walnut St, Texarkana 71854 . . . . fax 870-779-2044

Institutional Release

Texarkana Regional Correctional Facility—ADC	870-779-3939
305 E. 5th St, Texarkana 71854	fax 870-779-1616

Area 13
Offices

El Dorado Area Office	870-862-3449
1812 Lorene St., El Dorado 71730	fax 870-862-8725
Camden Office	870-837-1140
232 North Adams Ave., Camden 71701	fax 870-837-1308
Fordyce Office	870-352-8404
106 S. Charlotte St., Fordyce 71742	fax 870-352-3111
Magnolia Office	870-234-6016
222 South Pine St., Magnolia 71753	fax 870-234-6246

For further details or updates:
http://www.dcc.arkansas.gov/locations_area_offices_offices.html

COUNTY JAILS

Arkansas County Jail
     1000 Rice Belt Ave., De Witt 72042 870-946-1421

Ashley County Jail
     842 Ashley 12 W., Hamburg 71646 870-853-2040

Baxter County Jail
     904 Highway 62 W., Mountain Home 72653 870-425-7000

Benton County Jail
     1300 SW 14th St., Bentonville 72712 479-271-1011

Boone County Jail
     5800 Law Dr., Harrison 72601 870-429-1406

Bradley County Sheriff (uses Ashley jail)
     101 East Cedar St., Warren 71671 870-226-3491

Calhoun County Jail
     449 9th, Hampton 72503 870-798-2323

Carroll County Jail
     205 Hailey Road, Berryville 72616 870-423-2297

Chicot County Jail
     514 Church Street, Lake Village 71653 870-265-5536

Clark County Jail
     406 South 5th St., Arkadelphia 72470 870-246-2222

Clay County Jail
     268 South 2nd Ave., Piggott 72454 870-598-2270

Cleburne County Detention Center
     914 South 9th St., Heber Springs 72543 501-362-2596

Cleveland County Jail
     20 Magnolia, Rison 71665 870-325-6222

Columbia County Sheriff Detention Facility
     82 Magnolia 300, Magnolia 71753 870-234-5331

Conway County Detention Center
30 Southern Valley Dr., Morrilton 72110 501-354-9627

Craighead County Detention
901 Willett Road, Jonesboro 72401 870-933-4526

Crawford County Detention Center
317 Main Street, Van Buren 72956.. 479-474-1721

Crittenden County Jail
350 Afco Road, West Memphis 72301 870-702-2051

Cross County Detention Center
705 East Union Ave., Wynne 72396 870-238-5784

Dallas County Jail
106 S. Charlotte St., P.O. Box 689, Fordyce 71742 870-352-2002

Desha County Jail
604 President St., Arkansas City 71630 870-877-2327

Drew County Jail
106 South Main St., Monticello 71655 870-460-6215

Faulkner County Jail
Unit 1, Courthouse, 801 Locust St., Conway 72032. 501-450-4914
Unit 2, 500 S. German Lane, Conway 72032. 501-328-4160

Franklin County Jail
101 East Main, Charleston 72933 479-667-4127

Fulton County Jail
114 West Locust, Salem 72576 870-895-2601

Garland County Adult Detention
525 Ouachita Avenue, Hot Springs 71901 501-622-3683

Grant County Sheriff Jail (Sheridan P.D.)
304 Gatzke Drive, Sheridan 72150 870-942-5512

Greene County Jail
1809 N. Rockingchair Rd., Paragould 72450 870-236-7612

Hempstead County Jail
     312 S. Washington St., Hope 71801 870-777-6727

Hot Spring County Jail
     215 East Highland Ave., Malvern 72104. 501-865-2900

Howard County Detention Center
     101 Isaac Perkins Blvd., Nashville 71852 870-845-2626

Independence County Jail
     569 West Main St., Batesville 72503 870-612-6880

Izard County Detention Facility
     300 Circle Dr., Melbourne 72556 870-368-4203

Jackson County Jail
     617 Second Street, Newport 72112 870-523-5842

Jefferson County Jail
     300 East 2nd Ave., Pine Bluff 71601 870-541-5488

Johnson County Jail
     301 Porter Industrial Rd, Clarksville 72830 479-754-2200

Lafayette County Jail
     #5 Courthouse Square, Lewisville 71845 870-921-4252

Lawrence County Jail
     315 West Main St., Walnut Ridge 72476 870-886-2525

Lee County Jail
     East Arkansas Regional Unit–ADC
     326 Lee County Road 601, Brickeys 72320. 870-295-7777

Lincoln County Detention Center
     300 South Drew St., Star City 71667 870-628-4217

Little River County Jail
     351 N. 2nd St., Ashdown 71822 870-898-5115

Logan County Jail
     508 West Grober St., Paris 72855 479-963-3271

Lonoke County Jail
      440 DeeDee Lane, Lonoke 72086.......................... 501-676-6494 ext 2

Madison County Jail
      #1 Main St., Huntsville 72740............................. 479-738-2320

Marion County Jail
      491 Highways 62 & 412 W., Yellville 72687................. 870-449-4236

Miller County Jail
      2300 East Street, Texarkana 71854........................ 870-779-3611

Mississippi County Jail
      685 N. County Rd 599, Luxora 72358-4808.................. 870-762-2243

Monroe County Jail
      200 South Main Street, Clarendon 72029................... 870-747-3811

Montgomery County Jail
      105 Highway 270 E, Mount Ida 71957...................... 870-867-3151

Nevada County Jail
      215 East 2nd St South, Prescott 71857.................... 870-887-2616

Newton County Jail
      300 Spring St., Jasper 72641................... (NCSO) 870-446-5124

Ouachita County Jail
      145 Scott Alley SW, Camden 71701........................ 870-837-2200

Perry County Jail
      106 North Oak St., Perryville 72126..................... 501-889-2333

Phillips County Jail
      205 Perry St., Helena 72342............................. 870-338-5560

Pike County Jail
      305 Industrial Park, Murfreesboro 71958................. 870-285-3315

Poinsett County Jail
      1500 Justice Drive, Harrisburg 72432 870-578-5411

Polk County Jail
      507 Church Avenue, Mena 71953........................... 479-394-2511

Pope County Jail
      100 West Main, Russellville 72801 479-968-2558

Prairie County Jail
      200 Des Arc Lake Rd, Des Arc 72040. 870-256-4764

Pulaski County Detention Center
      3201 W. Roosevelt Rd, Little Rock 72204. 501-340-7000
      http://www.pcso.org/InmateRoster.shtml
   Northside Book-In (closed during 2012; could reopen someday)
      315 W. 29th, North Little Rock 72114. 501-791-7252

Randolph County Jail
      1510 Pace Road, Pocahontas 72455 870-892-8888

Saline County Detention Center
      735 S. Neeley Street, Benton 72015. 501-303-5642

Scott County Jail
      100 W. 1st St., Box 13, Waldron 72958 479-637-4155

Searcy County Jail
      208 Factory Road, Marshall 72650 870-448-2340

Sebastian County Jail
      800 South A St., Fort Smith 72901 479-783-1051

Sevier County Jail
      137 West Robinson Road, De Queen 71832. 870-642-2125

St. Francis County Jail
      313 S. Izard St. Forrest City 72335. 870-633-2611

Sharp County Jail
      30A Court Street, Hardy 72513 870-994-7329

Stone County Jail
      1009 Sheriff's Dr., Mountain View 72560. 870-269-3825

Washington County Jail
      1155 W. Clydesdale Dr, Fayetteville 72701. 479-444-5830

Union County Jail
      250 American Road, El Dorado 71730 870-864-1990

Van Buren County Jail
184 Detention Drive, Clinton 72031.............................. 501-745-4444

White County Jail
1600 East Booth Road, Searcy 72143 501-279-6279

Woodruff County Jail
500 North 3rd Street, Augusta 72006 870-347-5152

Yell County Jail
101 East 5th Street, Danville 72833 479-495-2811
106 Union Street, Dardanelle 72834 479-229-4175

CITY JAILS
(Source: Arkansas Criminal Detention Facilities Review Board)

201 W. Walnut Street	870-762-0405
Blytheville 72315.	fax 870-762-0425
497 E. Main	479-675-3508
Booneville 72927.	fax 479-675-3899
233 W. Cedar Street	870-734-3434
Brinkley 72021.	fax 870-734-1333
101 N. Second Street, P.O. Box 1113	501-843-6526
Cabot 72023.	fax 501-843-5437
122 Main Street, P.O. Box 49	870-552-7893
Carlisle 72024.	fax 870-552-3677
1105 Prairie Street	501-450-6120
Conway 72032.	fax 501-328-4102
308 W. Main Street, P.O. Box 538	870-857-3311
Corning 72422.	fax 870-857-6506
307 Main Street, P.O. Box 560	870-364-4131
Crossett 71635.	fax 870-857-6506
2005 State Hwy. 22, P.O. Box 696	479-229-2533
Dardanelle 72834.	fax 479-229-1613
112 N. Freeman, P.O. Box 371	870-538-5269
Dermott 71638.	fax 870-538-5400
149 E. Waterman Street, P.O. Box 157	870-382-5511
Dumas 71639.	fax 870-382-5838
110 N.W. Second Street, P.O. Box 249	501-842-1586
England 72046.	fax 501-842-9249
147 Passion Play Rd.	479-853-8666
Eureka Springs 72632.	fax 479-253-2006
101 S. Main	870-352-2178
Fordyce 71742.	fax 870-352-8187

225 N. Rosser Street	870-633-3434
Forrest City 72335.	fax 870-261-1421
210 N. Second Street	870-356-3333
Glenwood 71943.	fax 870-261-1421
103 E. Maple Street	870-353-2211
Gurdon 71743..	fax 870-353-5202
116 S. Spring Street, P.O. Box 1715	870-741-5463
Harrison 72601..	fax 870-741-1678
98 E. Plaza Street	870-572-3442
Helena-West Helena 72390.	fax 870-572-9093
704 W. Commerce Street	870-670-5113
Horseshoe Bend 72512	fax 870-670-4358
1412 W. Main Street	501-982-3191
Jacksonville 72076	fax 501-982-0505
114 N. Chicot St	870-265-5055
Lake Village 71653.	Jail fax 870-265-4745
113 S. Greenwood Ave., P.O. Box 610	870-475-2566
Lepanto 72354.	fax 870-475-3566
203 W. Front Street	501-676-6953
Lonoke 72086.	fax 501-676-6973
16 Court Street	870-295-2508
Marianna 72360.	fax 870-295-7878
1 Elm Street	870-358-2024
Marked Tree 72365.	fax 870-358-7867
100 Millwood Circle	501-851-1337 ext 107
Maumelle 72113..	fax 501-851-3875
2412 Hwy. 65 N, P.O. Box 135	870-222-3636
McGehee 71654.	fax 870-222-4859
212 N. Moose	501-354-0131
Morrilton 72110.	fax 501-354-3104

401 W. Keiser	870-563-5213
Osceola 72370.	fax 870-563-5657
407 S. Stewart	870-595-2423
Rector 72461.	fax 870-595-2186
1905 S. Dixieland Road	479-621-1172
Rogers 72758.	fax 479-986-3645
304 Gatzke Drive	870-942-4642
Sheridan 72150..	fax 870-942-4015
2201 E. Kiehl Ave	501-835-1425
Sherwood 72120.	fax 501-835-2484
410 N. Broadway, P.O. Box 80	479-524-4118
Siloam Springs 72761.	fax 479-524-6915
201 N. Spring Street	479-750-8543
Springdale 72764.	fax 479-750-8553
100 N. Melton Ave	870-483-6423
Trumann 72472..	fax 870-483-2996
200 Alabama Street	870-226-3703
Warren 71671	fax 870-226-3300

JUVENILE CORRECTION AND SERVICES
http://www.state.ar.us/dhs/dys/dys_provider_directory.html

State Juvenile Correctional Facilities
(and contractors)

G4S Youth Services, LLC
9609 Gayton Road, Suite 100
Richmond, VA 23238
804-754-1100
fax 804-741-9515

Arkansas Juvenile Assessment and
Treatment Center
1501 Woody Drive
Alexander 72002
501-682-9800
fax 501-682-9801

South Arkansas Youth Servs.
P.O. Box 2058
Magnolia 71754
870-234-6550
fax 870-234-3822

Dermott Correctional Facility
878 East Gaines Street
Dermott 71638
870-538-0223
fax 870-538-5096

County Juvenile Detention Centers

Arkansas County JDC
1010 Rice Belt Rd
Dewitt 72042. 870-946-8411
fax 870-946-1715

Benton County JDC
203 E. Central
Bentonville 72712. 479-271-1713
dcottrell@co.benton.ar.us
fax 479-271-1716

Craighead County JDC
901 Willett Rd.
Jonesboro 72401. 870-933-4578
tkoons@craigheadso.org
fax 879-933-4524

Crittendon County JDC
350 Afco Rd.
W Memphis 72301. 870-702-2067
ccn642@yahoo.com
fax 870-702-2015

Faulkner County JDC
801 Locust St
Conway 72032. 501-450-4914
                                                                      fax 501-450-4949

Garland County JDC
222 Woodbine
Hot Springs 71901. 501-622-3643
bcoz@garlandcounty.org   fax 501-622-3646

Jefferson County JDC
301 E 2d Ave
Pine Bluff 71601.. 870-541-8502
lajjjc2003@yahoo.com

Miller County JDC
2200 Bankes Rd
Texarkana 71854. 870-773-3776
tyna827@aol.com   fax 870-772-4438

Mississippi County JDC
685 N County Rd 599
Luxora 72358. 870-658-2242
stacie_bryant2001@yahoo.com   fax 870-658-2510

Pulaski County JDC
3001 W Roosevelt Rd.
Little Rock, Ar. 72204.. 501-340-6697
cgardner@co.pulaski.ar.us   fax 501-340-6888

Sebastian County JDC
801 South A Street
Fort Smith 72901. 479-783-3532
fhall@co.sebastian.ar.us   fax 479-784-1532

Washington County JDC
885 Clydesdale Rd
Fayetteville 72701. . . . . .479-444-1670 ext. 21
jmack@co.washington.ar.us   fax 479-444-1675

White River JDC
105 County Yard Rd
Batesville 72501. 870-612-6814
pkendrick@suddenlinkmail.com   fax 870-612-6816

Yell County JDC
P.O. Box 1688
Danville 72833.. 479-495-7739
jackristi@arkwest.com   fax 479-495-7741

Community-Based Programs
(Judicial District map on page 1)

Comprehensive Juvenile
     Services, Inc.
Judicial Districts 12, 18W, 21
1606 South "J"
Fort Smith 72901
479-785-4031
fax 479-785-5354

Community Service, Inc.
Judicial Districts 5, 15, 20
100 South Cherokee
P.O. Box 679
Morrilton 72110
501-354-4589
fax 501-354-5410

East Arkansas Youth Services, Inc.
Judicial District 1
104 Cypress Street
Marion 72364
870-739-4219
fax 870-739-4479

Ouachita Children's Center
Judicial Districts 9E, 18E
339 Charteroak
P.O. Box 1180
Hot Springs 71901
501-623-5591
fax 501-623-4226

Consolidated Youth Services
Judicial Districts 2, 3
4220 Stadium Boulevard
Jonesboro 72404
870-972-1110
fax 870-972-5433

Counseling Clinic, Inc.
Judicial Districts 7, 22
307 Sevier Street
Benton 72015
501-315-4224
fax 501-776-0411

Health Resources of Arkansas, Inc.
Judicial Districts 16, 17
1800 Myers Street
P.O. Box 2578
Batesville 72501
870-793-8925, 870-793-2311
fax 870-793-8929

Phoenix Youth & Family Services
Judicial District 10
310 North Alabama Street
P.O. Box 654
Crossett 71635
870-364-1676
fax 870-364-1779

Professional Counseling
Associates, Inc.
Judicial District 23
109 West Second Street
P.O. Box 438
Lonoke 72086
501-221-1843, 501-676-5968
fax 501-676-3152

SW AR Counseling & Mental
    Health Center
Judicial Districts 8N, 8S, 9W
2904 Arkansas Blvd.
P.O. Box 1987
Texarkana 75504
870-773-4655

Youth Bridge, Inc.
Judicial Districts 4, 14, 19E, 19W
3715 North Business Dr., Suite 109
Fayetteville 72703
479-575-9471
fax 479-575-9149

South Arkansas Youth Services, Inc.
Judicial District 13
124 South Jackson, Suite 308
P.O. Box 2058
Magnolia 71754
870-234-6550 ext. 306
fax 870-234-3822

United Family Services–Little Rock
Judicial Districts 6, 11E, 11W
715 West Second St.
Little Rock 72201
501-376-0111

Specialized Residential Program Directory

Centers for Youth & Families
Residential Psychiatric Treatment
6501 West 12th Street
Little Rock 72204
501-666-8686
fax 501-660-5433

Division of Behavioral Health
Arkansas State Hospital
Residential Sex Offender
    Treatment
4313 W. Markham
Little Rock 72205
501-686-9000
fax 501-686-9182

Consolidated Youth Services, Inc.
Residential Sex Offender Treatment
4220 Stadium Boulevard
Jonesboro 72404
870-972-1110
fax 870-972-5433

South AR Youth Services
Therapeutic Group Home
450 Columbia 11 E
P.O. Box 2058 (71753)
Magnolia 71754
870-234-6550
fax 870-234-3822

Piney Ridge Center, Inc.
Residential Sex Offender
Treatment
4253 N Crossover Road
Fayetteville 72703
479-587-1408
fax 479-587-1085

Vera Lloyd Presbyterian Home
and Family Services, Inc.
Therapeutic Group Home
745 Old Warren Road
Monticello 71655
870-367-9035
fax 870-367-9038

Corporate Office:
1501 N. University, Suite 345
Little Rock 72207
501-666-8195
fax 501-666-8198

UHS of Benton, Inc. dba Rivendell
Behavioral Health Services
Residential Psychiatric Treatment
100 Rivendell Drive
Benton 72015
501-316-1255
fax 501-794-0908

Youth Home, Inc.
Residential Psychiatric Treatment
20400 Colonel Glenn Road
Little Rock 72210
501-821-5500
fax 501-821-5580

Youth Bridge, Inc.
Substance Abuse Treatment
3715 N. Business Dr., # 109
Fayetteville 72703
479-575-9471

Youth Villages, Inc.
Residential Psychiatric Treatment
3320 Brother Blvd
Memphis, TN 38133
901-251-5000

Non-Residential Program Directory

Paul L. Deyoub, Ph.D., P.A.
Intake and Assessment
11219 Financial Park Pl., #210
Little Rock 72211
501-224-8819
fax 501-224-6355

UAMS – Department of Pediatrics
Sex Offender Assessment, Treatment and Casework Services
4301 West Markham St.
P.O. Box 250960 (72225)
Little Rock 72205
501-364-5262
fax 501-364-3418

Juvenile Treatment Center Directory

Consolidated Youth Services, Inc.
4220 Stadium Boulevard
Jonesboro 72404
870-972-1110
fax 870-972-5433

Harrisburg Juvenile Treatment Center
1800 Pine Grove Lane
Harrisburg 72432
870-578-5886

South Arkansas Youth Center
P.O. Box 2058
Magnolia 71754
870-234-6550

Colt Juvenile Treatment Center
1388 SFC 118
Colt 72326
870-633-6467
fax 870-633-6732

Mansfield Juvenile Treatment
Services
P.O. Box 487
Mansfield 72944
479-928-0166
fax 479-928-2060

Mansfield Juvenile Treatment Center
for Girls
P.O. Box 416
Mansfield 72944
479-928-5178
fax 479-928-5195

Dermott Juvenile Treatment Center
P.O. Box 142
Dermott 71638
870-538-3400
fax 870-538-3446

Lewisville Juvenile Treatment Center
P.O. Box 723
Lewisville 71638
870-921-5302
fax 870-921-5305

JJDP Sub-Grantee Program Directory

Baxter County Juvenile Services
Deinstitutionalization of Status
Offenders
312 Bomber Blvd.
Mountain Home 72653
870-425-3840
fax 870-424-2955

East Arkansas Youth Services, Inc.
104 Cypress Street
Marion 72364
870-739-4219
fax 870-739-4479

Garland County Juvenile Detention Ctr.
Mental Health Services
222 Woodbine
Hot Springs 71901
501-662-3643
fax 501-321-4212

Jefferson County
Pine Bluff 71601
870-541-5455

Phoenix Youth & Family
         Services, Inc.
310 N. Alabama St.
Crossett 71635
870-364-1676
fax 870-364-1779

Scotty Scholl Communications
611 Edswood Road
Little Rock 72223
501-448-0030
fax 501-448-0030

Sixth Judicial Dist. Juvenile Ct.
3001 West Roosevelt
Little Rock 72204
501-340-6731
fax 501-340-7011

United Family Services, Inc.
P.O. Box 5408
Pine Bluff 71611
870-534-3386
fax 870-534-3386

Holman Community Development Corp.
Delinquency Prevention
605 North Buerkle
Stuttgart 72160
870-673-9166
fax 870-673-9166 (call first)

Magnolia Public Schools
1400 High School Drive
Magnolia 71753
870-234-4933

Pulaski County Youth Services
Juvenile Pre-trial services
201 S. Broadway, Suite 220
Little Rock 72201
501-340-8250
fax 501-340-8259

Simone's Home, Inc. (girls)
Little Rock
501-772-4987

TOPPS, Inc. (girls)
3512 West 2nd
Pine Bluff 71601
870-850-7377
fax 870-850-7366

Youth Home, Inc.
20400 Colonel Glenn Road
Little Rock 72210
501-821-5500
fax 501-821-5580

FEDERAL

U.S. BUREAU OF PRISONS
http://www.bop.gov/

Unit locations. . . . . http://www.bop.gov/

Inmate locator. http://www.bop.gov/iloc2/LocateInmate.jsp

U.S. MARSHAL'S PRETRIAL DETENTION FACILITIES
Note: Marshal's office addresses and numbers listed under both Federal Courts and Law Enforcement; see county jails for address and phone number of pretrial detention facilities.

Eastern District:

Dallas County Jail
Faulkner County Jail
Lonoke County Jail
Jefferson County Jail
Pulaski County Regional Detention Facility
Saline County Jail
Sheridan Detention Center
Van Buren County Jail
White County Jail

occasionally:
>   West Tennessee Detention Facility (mostly awaiting airlift)
>   Corrections Corporation of America
>   6299 Finde Naifeh Dr., P.O. Box 509. 901-294-3060
>   Mason, TN 38049. . . . . fax 901-294-2936
>   Support Center:
>   10 Burton Hills Blvd. 800-624-2931
>   Nashville, TN 37215. . . . . fax 615-263-3140
>   Craighead County Jail

Western District:

Benton County
Bowie County Correctional (occasionally)
>   105 W Front St.
>   Texarkana, TX 75501 903-798-3505
Garland County (overnight)
Miller County
Sebastian County

Texarkana City Jail
    Bi-State Criminal Justice Center
    100 North Stateline Ave.
    Texarkana, TX 75501.................................... 903-798-3199
Union County
Washington County

U.S. PROBATION OFFICES

http://www.uscourts.gov/FederalCourts/ProbationPretrialServices.aspx

Eastern District of Arkansas:

Main office
A228 U.S. Courthouse
600 West Capitol Ave. Ste. 233
Little Rock 72201
501-604-5240
fax 501-324-5641

321 Federal Building
615 S. Main St.
Jonesboro 72401
870-935-1510
fax 870-935-4977

3113 Federal Building
100 E. 8th St.
Pine Bluff 71601
870-536-4130
fax 870-534-8498

Western District of Arkansas:

307 U.S. P.O. & Courthouse
101 South Jackson
El Dorado 71730
800-282-5920
870-862-1347

316 Federal Building
35 East Mountain
Fayetteville 72701
800-282-5918
479-442-9892

1063 U.S. Courthouse
30 S. 6th St.
P.O. Box 1564 (72902)
Ft. Smith 71901
800-282-5919
479-783-8050
fax 479-783-5761

308 Federal Building
100 Reserve
P.O. Box 6199 (71903)
Hot Springs 71901
800-262-5875
501-321-9526
fax 501-321-2689

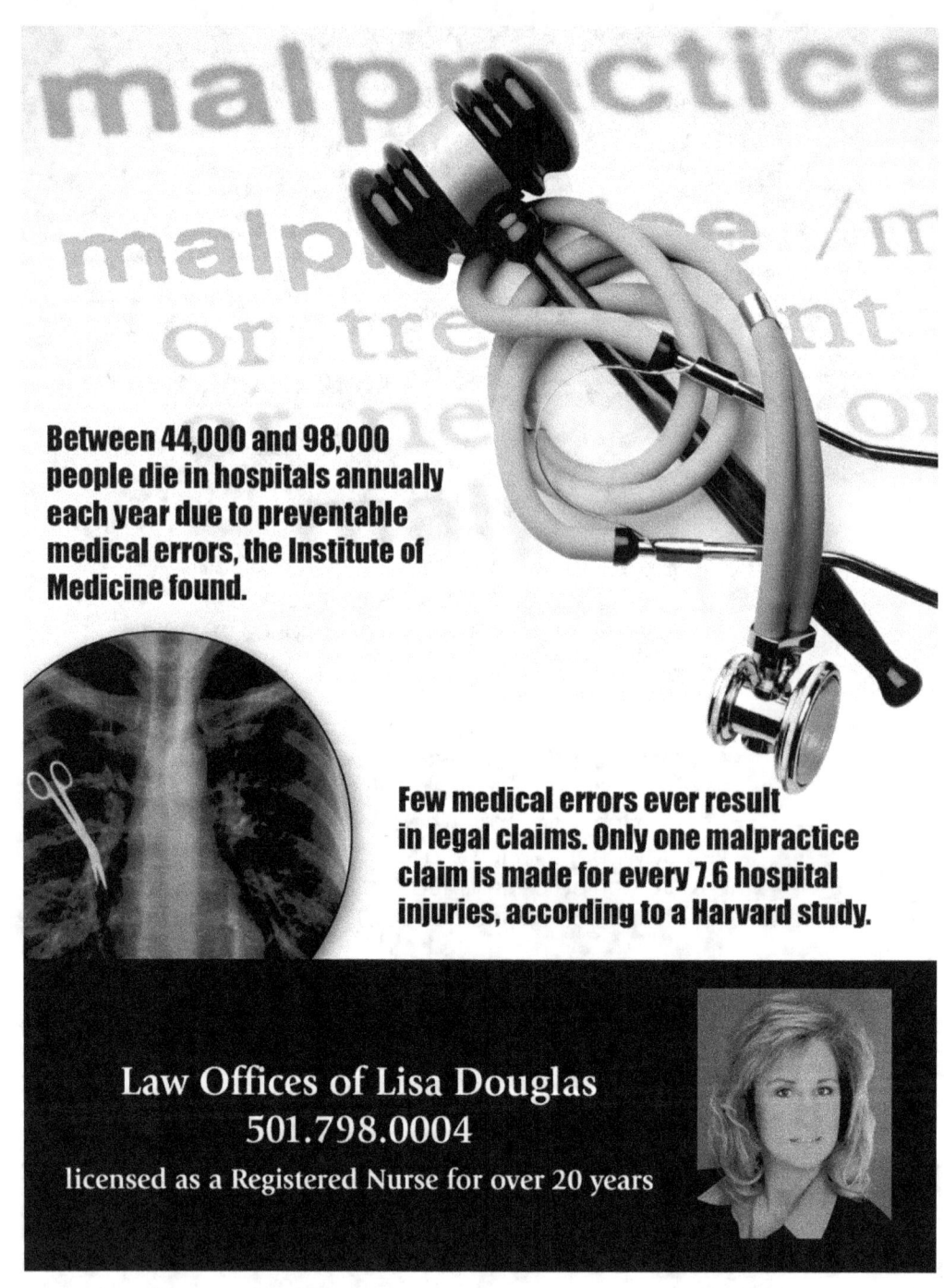

The first ten amendments to the Constitution are the Bill of Rights, and they were adopted in 1791 to limit government power against individuals. The Fourth Amendment protects "the people" against arbitrary invasions by the police into into the security of their persons and property.

The law favors any search under a search warrant. "The point of the Fourth Amendment, which often is not grasped by zealous officers, is not that it denies law enforcement the support of the usual inferences which reasonable men draw from evidence. Its protection consists in requiring that those inferences be drawn by a neutral and detached magistrate instead of being judged by the officer engaged in the often competitive enterprise of ferreting out crime." Johnson v. United States, 333 U.S. 10, 13-14 (1948). Once a search warrant issues, it is presumed valid.

The protections of the Fourth Amendment can be claimed by the guilty, the innocent, the sinner, or the saint.

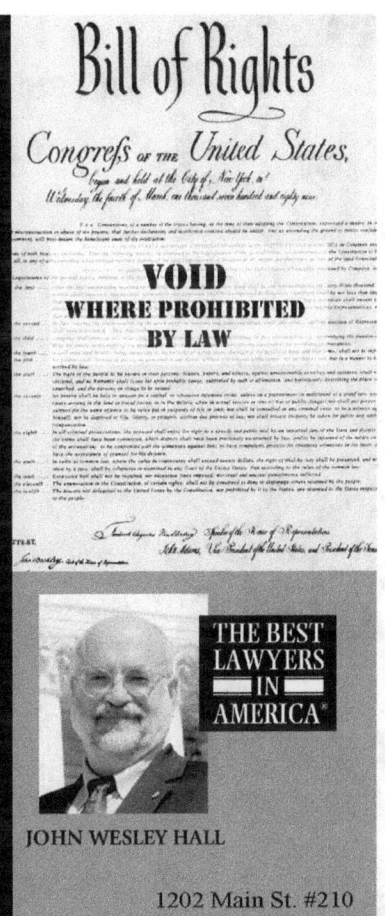

JOHN WESLEY HALL

1202 Main St. #210
Little Rock, AR 72202
501.371.9131

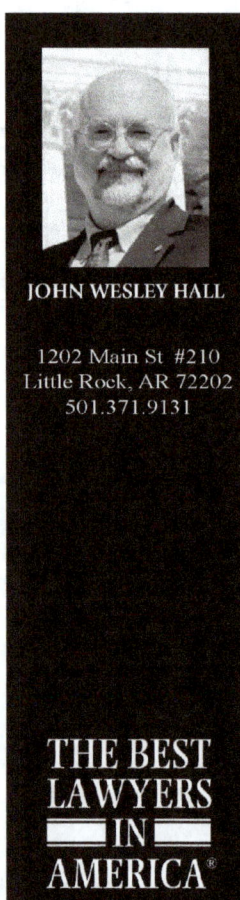

JOHN WESLEY HALL

1202 Main St #210
Little Rock, AR 72202
501.371.9131

THE BEST
LAWYERS
═══IN═══
AMERICA®

**The Constitution guarantees
the presumption of
innocence
and proof beyond a
reasonable doubt**

This is the genius of the common law
system of trial by jury. The defense
does not have to do a thing at the trial,
and the person accused cannot be
made to testify. The presumption of
innocence alone is enough to require
acquittal if the prosecution does
not persuade the jury of guilt beyond
a reasonable doubt.

NOTES

NOTES

PARTIAL INDEX
by subject matter; no persons

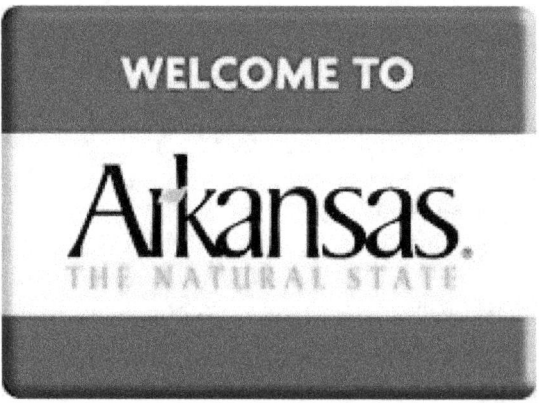

**Come on vacation,
don't leave on probation**

Call John Wesley Hall
501-371-9131
Criminal Defense Lawyer

The best defense is not cheap

A criminal defense lawyer's value is
in considering what's at stake,
something you might not have done in the first place